The U.S. Presidency

Table of Contents

The U.S. Presidency:

An Introduction

Today, after over two hundred years of American history, the office of the president of the United States is the most powerful political office in the world. The American president serves as the chief executive of the world's largest, and most productive economy and is commander in chief of one of the most powerful and technologically advanced militaries in history.

In today's global economy, whoever serves as America's president makes decisions which shape the lives, not only of the citizens of the United States, but of people in every hemisphere.

American presidents have not always wielded such power. Over two centuries ago, the United States Constitution redefined the structure of American government. This important document divided national power into three branches—the legislative branch (embodied in the Congress, which makes federal laws), the judicial branch (embodied in the federal court system, which interprets the laws), and the executive branch, which vests proscribed powers in the president.

While in 1789—at the time of the signing of the Constitution into law—the power of the presidency (in its infancy) did not extend beyond the boundaries of the United States, over the ensuing decades and centuries, the presidency grew, expanding its sphere of influence to one of global preeminence.

Throughout these pages, we will trace the complicated evolution of the American presidency. We will examine the distinct legacies and unique contributions of the extraordinary men who have held this most prestigious office since 1789, and discuss the powerful convergence of personality and circumstance which transformed the office of our nation's chief executive into the most powerful political office in the world.

Some of the men featured in this book were powerful leaders who reshaped the dimension and scope of presidential power.

The Men Who Served Their Country

Some of their names are well known even to casual students of history. Men such as George Washington, Thomas Jefferson, Andrew Jackson, Abraham Lincoln, Woodrow Wilson, Franklin Roosevelt, and Ronald Reagan brought strong personalities to their role as president.

Others brought less personality, less success, and less change to the office. Some names are less known to us. Men such as Millard Fillmore, Franklin Pierce, Zachary Taylor, William Henry Harrison, and his grandson Benjamin Harrison had little impact on the presidency.

At times, the historical circumstances of a president's term gave shape to his leadership. Abraham Lincoln, for example, a witty and wise lawyer from Illinois, became one of the greatest of American presidents because he led the northern states to victory in the Civil War. Other wartime presidents such as Woodrow Wilson and Franklin Roosevelt rose to greatness by meeting the challenge of international conflict. Others are remembered because they used the power of the presidency to change public policy or to rescue the nation from economic crisis.

Not only does the president have the power to enforce laws, he may also encourage the formation of new laws. Typically, in a president's State of the Union message, delivered to Congress every January, he will suggest a legislative program. By this suggestion, he makes it clear to Congress what laws he would like enacted.

When proposed laws reach the desk of the president which he does not like, he holds the power to veto them. If he vetoes a proposed bill, he sends it back to Congress. They may override his veto by a two-thirds vote.

Additional powers of the president include the ability to pardon any citizen of the United States of a crime, with the exception of impeachment. He may also grant a postponement of a punishment.

Although political parties did not officially exist when the Constitution was written, the president is now viewed as the leader of his political party. He may use that power to appoint members of his political party to government positions, or help set the party's national agenda.

Despite the powers held by the president, he does not carry out his duties alone. Presidents rely on hundreds of advisors—experts who understand complex issues and subjects and can communicate these to the chief executive.

Among a president's most important advisors are those who serve as heads of cabinet departments. Although the Constitution does not mention a "cabinet" by name, the first such advisors were created in 1789 and included a secretary of foreign affairs, a secretary of war, a secretary of the treasury, and an attorney general.

Over the years, other cabinet positions have been added. Today, they include the departments of state, treasury, defense, justice, interior, agriculture, commerce, labor, health and human services, education, housing and urban development, transportation, energy, and veterans affairs.

The Diversity of the Presidency

For over two centuries the American people have elected a president every four years. Elections take place on the first Tuesday after the first Monday of November. By exercising their right to vote, American men and women have elected 43 men who have served in the office of the president.

They held the office for varying lengths of time from William Henry Harrison (elected in 1840)—who served only one month—to Franklin Delano Roosevelt [1933-1945]—who held the presidency for over 12 years. (No president will ever be in office for as many consecutive years as FDR. The 22nd Amendment to the Constitution—ratified in 1951—now limits presidents to two terms or a total of ten years.)

Each man made his mark on the presidency regardless of the length of his term. But who were these men? What can we say about those who

have been elected to the highest office in the land? What do they have in common? How different were they from one another? How did each man serve as a representative of his time?

One of the easiest observations to make about the men who served as president is that each one was unique. While all were American citizens who resided in the United States for at least 14 years as required by the Constitution, and all were white males, there are few other traits that they shared equally.

Historians predict that within the next generation, Americans will elect either a woman or a minority person as president.

While the Constitution specifies that a person must be at least 35 years of age to serve as president, the ages of the presidents vary widely. Examining their ages on the day they entered the presidency, the record shows that, including Bill Clinton, eight men were in their 40s, ten in their 60s, and a majority of 25 were in their 50s.

The youngest president was Theodore Roosevelt who was 42 when President McKinley was assassinated in 1901, thrusting Roosevelt into the presidency. The oldest was Ronald Reagan who turned 70 just weeks after his inauguration.

Thirty-two presidents were college educated. More attended Harvard than any other university or college. Most of the presidents were lawyers by profession. Some were farmers or planters. Others were soldiers. In fact, some men such as George Washington [1789–1797], Andrew Jackson [1829–1837], Ulysses Grant [1869–1877], and Dwight D. Eisenhower [1953–1961] were elected to the presidency almost entirely on their war record as commanding generals. A few were teachers or educators, including Woodrow Wilson and Lyndon Johnson. One, Andrew Johnson, was a tailor.

Typically, the presidents of the United States have been members of organized political parties. Early presidents belonged to political parties which do not exist today such as the Federalists, Democratic-Republicans, and Whigs. Most of the presidents belonged to either the Republican Party (17) or Democratic Party (14). Only one—

George Washington—did not belong to a political party at all.

Coming from All Corners of America

The men who have served as president have come from all regions of the country. Of the first twelve presidents, seven came from Virginia—one of the thirteen original colonies. Others have hailed from other southern states, such as Carter's Georgia or Clinton's Arkansas. Seven presidents have come from Ohio and five from New York. Texas, California, New Jersey, and Pennsylvania, are among other states that were homes to other presidents.

Throughout this study, we will focus on the men who have served as president—men who came from many different walks of life, each adding his distinct legacy to the history of the American presidency.

Review and Write

1. What do you think are the three most significant responsibilities of the president of the United States?

_____

_____

_____

2. Do you have favorite presidents? Who are they? Whom do you admire most among America's presidents? Why?

_____

_____

_____

_____

Young George Washington

His place in American history is certain, for few people have had a greater impact on America and the history of the early United States than George Washington. Often called the "Father of our Country," Washington remains a symbol of America's early leadership.

Planter, surveyor, military leader, politician, and patriot, he is a pivotal figure, integrally linked with the volatile transition from the colonial period to the American Revolution in which he took a leading role as commander of the Continental army. No other man made greater contributions or sacrificed more in the creation of the United States than did George Washington.

His legacy as a great American is sometimes complicated by myth. Many school children have heard the story of young George chopping down his father's prized cherry tree. When confronted, he confesses to his father that he is unable to lie—he had cut it down.

Another well-known tale features an athletic Washington throwing a silver dollar (in some stories a stone) across the broad expanse of the Rappahannock River. While such stories hyperbolize and aggrandize Washington's honesty and physical skill, they are assuredly not true.

Washington's life spanned most of the 18th century. He was born in Pope Creek's Farm in Westmoreland County, Virginia, on February 22, 1732. He was the oldest son of Augustine and Mary Ball Washington. (George had an elder half-brother, Lawrence, from an earlier marriage of Augustine's.)

George represented the fourth generation of Washingtons to live in America. His great-grandfather, John Washington, had settled in America in the 1600s by accident. John was a sailor on a small English sailing ship which ran aground in the Potomac River in 1656 or 1657. Through a lengthy stay, while his ship was under repair, he decided to remain in Virginia. His original landholdings included the estate later called Mount Vernon—Washington's adult home.

Young George grew up along the banks of the Potomac River. He probably attended school in nearby Fredericksburg to the south. In his early years, he studied mathematics, surveying, the rules of manners fitting a gentleman, and classic literature. He wrote his lessons out on heavy paper which his mother sewed into notebooks. Washington's studies, however, were not extensive. He probably attended school until the age of 14 or 15. His father had probably made plans for George to attend school in England, but he died when George was only 11.

During his teenage years, George Washington developed into a well-rounded young man. He learned to dance, and enjoyed fox hunts and boating on the Potomac River. He helped his half-brother Lawrence who had inherited their father's estate at Mount Vernon. The two brothers were always very close.

One of young Washington's early adventures was a surveying expedition at age 16. The month-long survey of Lord Fairfax—a wealthy Virginia neighbor—took Washington inland to western Virginia. Weeks of sleeping outdoors, hunting for food, and earning money as a surveying assistant gave Washington a sense of having grown up. (While on the expedition, he began shaving.)

As Washington developed into a strong, young man, he began to take on the impressive physical appearance for which he was known. He stood straight and tall, and grew to a height of over 6 feet 2 inches. Washington was broad-shouldered and well-built. A friend wrote of Washington in his 20s, "He may be described as being straight as an Indian . . . and weighing 175 pounds . . . A large and straight rather than prominent nose; blue-gray penetrating eyes and dark brown hair." The same description indicates that Washington was easily sunburned.

Over the next few years, Washington was hired to complete several surveys. He helped survey the land which would later become the city of Alexandria, Virginia. Carefully, he saved his money and bought additional land for himself. By age 18, he owned 1500 new acres of land.

At age 20, Washington faced a tragic loss. His brother, Lawrence, died in 1752. Not long afterwards—perhaps inspired by the stories

Lawrence had told about his own military service—George applied for a commission in the Virginia colonial militia. With no military experience to his credit, George studied books on military tactics and training.

In 1753, Washington received orders from Virginia Governor Robert Dinwiddie to deliver a message to the French commandant at Fort Le Boeuf in the Ohio River Valley. (Both the English and the French claimed the Ohio Valley.) Dinwiddie's message was a warning to the French not to erect future forts in the British-claimed region. With six comrades, Washington delivered the message, but was rebuffed.

The trip to and from Fort Le Boeuf was treacherous for young Washington. Traveling as many as 20 miles a day, he and his companions braved rugged terrain, icy rivers, and bitter cold. Washington met with Indians in the region and, on one occasion, was almost killed. He nearly drowned on a raft one day while crossing the Allegheny River. Such trials provided Washington with experience to meet the challenges he would face later in life.

Review and Write

1. What roles did Washington fulfill which helped make him the "Father of our Country"?

2. How did Washington's family arrive in America in the 1600s?

3. Give Washington's physical description.

Washington and the Revolution

Although George Washington's mission to warn the French out of the Ohio Valley failed, Virginia's governor was not yet finished with the young Virginian. He sent George back into the Ohio wilderness to erect a fort to defy the French in the region.

In April 1754, while in the wilderness of western Pennsylvania, Washington encountered a party of French Canadians and their Indian allies. Surprising the French, Washington's Indian comrade, Half King, killed the French leader, a commander known as the Sieur de Jumonville.

Later, while erecting his own fort at Great Meadows, Pennsylvania (known as Fort Necessity), Washington was promoted to the rank of colonel in the Virginia militia. By early June, he and his men were reinforced by 180 additional Virginia militiamen and a small number of Native Americans. Less than two weeks later, 100 British soldiers arrived to provide additional support and additional supplies.

The next month, before his fort was completed, Washington and his army of fewer than 400 men were attacked by the French. The daylong battle took place in heavy rain. Outnumbered and low on food and ammunition, Washington surrendered to the French, suffering casualties of more than 100.

When Washington surrendered, he was forced to sign a document admitting he had killed a French ambassador—the Sieur de Jumonville. As news of the assassination spread to Europe, France and England soon found themselves at war.

Known as the French and Indian War (in Europe, it was called the Seven Years' War), this conflict ultimately decided which nation would control the Ohio River valley. But not before Washington participated in the expedition of British general, Edward Braddock, in the Pennsylvania wilderness.

When Braddock was attacked by French and Indians in the summer of 1755, Washington fought bravely. He wrote later how he luckily escaped without a wound, "though I had four bullets through my coat and two horses shot under me."

Following Braddock's defeat in the wilderness, Washington was promoted to colonel and was appointed commander in chief of all Virginia militia troops. He continued to fight in the French and Indian War, and witnessed the defeat of the French

at Fort Duquesne on the Ohio River.

With the defeat of the French at Fort Duquesne, Washington was reassigned by Governor Dinwiddie. He took up a command of Virginia colonial troops to provide defense of Virginia's frontier borders. Washington saw little action while serving in this region over the next few years. Although he continually called for renewed campaigns to force the surrender of Fort Duquesne, the British postponed the attack until 1758. Washington accompanied the 800-man force sent into the Ohio Valley wilderness. After an attack by Indians and French, which resulted in the deaths of 300 British troops, Washington and the others reached Fort Duquesne in November only to find the charred remains of the installation. The French had already burned it and fled to Canada.

Just weeks later, in December 1758, Washington resigned. His military experience had provided him with great knowledge concerning matters of war—information which served him well during his years as commander of the Continental army during the American Revolution.

In early 1759, he married the widow, Martha Dandridge Custis, who had inherited 17,000 acres and over a third of a million dollars. Over the next 16 years, Washington concentrated on building his fortune and adding to his landholdings. He added new buildings at Mount Vernon. These were years of peace and contentment for the Washingtons.

By 1769, Washington was a leader among Virginians opposed to England's policies of taxation on the colonies. From 1774 to 1775, he served as a delegate to the First and Second Continental Congress—an intercolonial body that organized the American protest of British policy.

When the events of Lexington and Concord led to the outbreak of war between the colonies and the Mother Country, Washington stepped forward and provided military leadership for the Continental army. The Second Continental Congress selected him as the army's commander in chief.

For the next eight years—from 1775 to 1783—Washington led a ragtag group of undernourished, underclothed, and sparsely-armed men against one of the greatest powers in the world. The general lost many more battles than he won. (Overall, his Revolutionary War record included three victories, eight losses, and one draw.) But Washington's greatness was his ability to sustain even a "raw militia, badly officered" against such an intimidating foe. As Washington's good friend, the French soldier and statesman, the Marquis de Lafayette wrote to him, ". . . if you were lost for America, there is nobody who could keep the army and Revolution for six months."

Among his important victories, the battle of Trenton is one of the best known. As the end of 1776 approached, many of Washington's soldiers were prepared to leave the army when their enlistments were complete. Desperately needing a victory to boost morale that winter, Washington ordered an early dawn attack against a garrison of German mercenaries—hired by the British to do their fighting—in Trenton, New Jersey.

While the famous painting by Emmanuel Leutze of Washington crossing the ice-choked waters of the Delaware River on Christmas night is not realistic—Washington did not stand during the crossing—his troops did surprise the groggy Germans, still drunk from their holiday celebrating, and won the battle. A second victory at Princeton soon followed. This victory helped keep Washington's army alive into 1777.

Review and Write

1. What long-range results did Washington's April 1754 encounter with the French have?

2. What activities did Washington concentrate on during the 1760s?

George Washington

1789–1797

Throughout the years of the Revolutionary War, General Washington under- stood his enemy. From prior experience, he knew that the British army moved slowly, and that he and his troops could survive by remaining a step ahead of them at all times.

Washington's crucial victory at Trenton was followed by another successful battle at neighboring Princeton in January 1777. But defeats dogged him through the year at Brandywine and Germantown, Pennsylvania. He and his army finished the year encamped at Valley Forge, where his men faced shortages of food, clothing, and shelter.

The next year brought renewed hope to the Continental army's commander. The French entered the American Revolution against the British in 1778, and provided much needed troops, supplies, money, and ships. During the summer of that year, Washington engaged the British near Monmouth Courheton, New Jersey, where he fought the British to a draw. His leadership during the fierce fight amid harsh summer heat (many men died of heat exhaustion during the battle) proved inspiring to his men.

Although Washington lost more battles than he won during the revolution, his dogged determination helped him maintain his army in the field. He managed to finally trap a significant British army in the small, tobacco port of Yorktown, Virginia, in the fall of 1781. With the help of the French army and navy (the French had entered the conflict on the patriot side in 1778) the battle of Yorktown proved to be Washington's greatest victory.

With the signing of the peace treaty in 1793, Washington again retired to his beloved lands at Mount Vernon. The next five years proved peaceful for the Virginia planter. He introduced new farming and animal breeding methods on his estate. He added to his estate by adding a greenhouse, an icehouse, and a mill. He traveled west and became interested in building canals on the frontier. For the most part, Washington steered clear of politics. He and Martha were celebrities, however, and received many visitors at their Mount Vernon estate.

By the late 1780s, however, it was becoming clear to many in the new United States that the country was suffering under a poorly constructed constitution known as the Articles of Confederation. By 1787, a convention was organized in Philadelphia to amend the Articles. Washington was elected to head the delegation from Virginia. At the convention, he was chosen as the meeting's president.

Throughout the summer of 1787, the convention turned its purpose to completely rewriting a new constitution rather than amending the Articles of Confederation. Under the new Constitution, the U.S. government created an executive branch headed by a president. When the states finally ratified the new Constitution in the summer of 1788, the stage was set for the election of Washington as America's first president. John Adams was to be his vice president.

Washington was inaugurated on April 30, 1789, in New York City. He stood on the balcony of Federal Hall at the corner of Broad and Wall streets, and swore to uphold and defend the Constitution as thousands of well-wishers looked on from the street below.

Since Washington was the first president, there was no official house yet to serve as the executive residence. He spent his entire presidency living in private homes in New York and Philadelphia. He and Martha spent many months at their home in Mount Vernon.

As president, Washington believed in a separation of the three branches of federal power—the executive, legislative, and judicial. He did not think it proper for him to influence the creation of new laws by Congress. Washington, however, was not beyond vetoing a bill if he thought it ill-advised.

By the fall of 1789, Congress established three departments to serve Washington—the departments of foreign affairs, war, and the treasury. Thomas Jefferson served as the first secretary of foreign affairs, Hamilton was the first secretary of the treasury, and Henry Knox headed the war department.

Although Washington did not favor dividing the country into political factions, he was not able to halt the early formation of political parties.

When Washington supported many of Hamilton's plans to stabilize the young American economy by creating a Bank of the United States and by excise taxes, he found himself criticized by the Democratic-Republicans who were loyal to Jefferson.

During Washington's first term, key steps were taken to strengthen the power of the newly formed federal government. A plan was devised to reduce the nation's long-standing debts, a national bank was established, and ambassadors were exchanged with several foreign nations. A census was taken in 1790 to establish the number of people living in America.

Following Washington's re-election in 1792, he faced his most serious foreign crisis. With England and France at war, Washington was pressured to

take America into the conflict. However, Washington refused, declaring the U.S. neutral.

In 1794, Washington faced the threat of domestic rebellion when western Pennsylvania farmers refused to pay their federal excise taxes on the whiskey they produced and sold. Ever the soldier, Washington led an army of 15,000 men into Pennsylvania to crush the so-called Whiskey Rebellion, but those involved had scattered long before Washington arrived.

During Washington's second term, two key treaties were negotiated—Jay's Treaty (1794), which addressed trade between the U.S. and England and called for the British to evacuate the last of their forts in the Old Northwest, and Pinckney's Treaty (1795), which granted western Americans the right to ship produce to the Spanish-held port of New Orleans tax free.

When Washington left office in 1797, he left a nation on solid footing—the nation's finances were stable, Indians in the Northwest Territory were subdued, and important foreign treaties had been signed. His final two years were spent at Mount Vernon where he died of a serious throat infection.

Review and Write

1. Summarize the contributions made by George Washington during the American Revolution.

_____

_____

_____

2. What serious crises did Washington face as the nation's first president?

_____

_____

_____

_____

_____

John Adams

1797–1801

Among America's Founding Fathers, John Adams was considered one of the most influential political leaders of his time. Long before he became the second president of the United States, Adams had already established his place in American history.

John Adams was born in Quincy, Massachusetts, (known at that time as Braintree) on October 30, 1735. The house of his birth still stands today. He represented the sixth generation of his family in colonial Massachusetts. His father was a church deacon, farmer, and militia officer. His mother's family consisted of Boston merchants and physicians.

Both parents believed in education and young John became the first of his family to receive a college degree, graduating from Harvard in 1755. In 1764, Adams was married to Abigail Smith, a woman nine years younger. They had four children, three of whom lived into adulthood.

Abigail proved to be a wonderful complement to her husband. Although she had little formal schooling, she was literate and well-read. A vast collection of their letters to one another reveals a woman who was well informed on many subjects, including politics.

By the late 1760s, Adams was a leading lawyer in the city of Boston. During those years, Adams participated in the revolutionary movement. He wrote a pamphlet denouncing the Stamp Act (1765) and became one of Massachusetts's leading patriots.

Yet when British soldiers opened fire on a taunting Boston mob in March of 1770 (the famous Boston Massacre), Adams chose to defend the soldiers at their trial. By doing so, he made clear his opposition to mob violence. During the trial, Adams argued that the soldiers involved in the alleged massacre were only guilty of following orders. Although he strongly endorsed the growing patriotic cause, he believed equally in justice. With Adams's defense, all but two of the British soldiers on trial for manslaughter were acquitted.

When Adams took the case of the British soldiers, he feared he would lose popularity with the people of Boston. But his fears were unfounded. Adams was soon selected as a delegate to the Continental Congress and served from 1774-1776. Adams supported the appointment of George Washington as commander of the Continental Army. In 1776, he helped draft the document known as the Declaration of Independence.

During the late 1770s and early 1780s, Adams served as a diplomatic minister to France. There, he and Benjamin Franklin convinced the French to support the Americans in their revolution against England. In 1782, Adams was appointed to negotiate the peace treaty ending the Revolutionary War and granting independence for the new United States.

As the young United States began charting its

course as a new nation, Adams continued to play a role. In 1785, he became the first U.S. minister to Great Britain. These were difficult years for him. His attempts to draft trade agreements with England largely failed, and he was often coolly received by the British. In 1788, Adams requested to step down, completing nearly a decade of service overseas to the United States government.

Almost immediately after his return to America, Adams was chosen to serve as the nation's first vice president under George Washington. This proved to be a role he did not enjoy, calling the vice-presidency the most insignificant office ever contrived. Adams was a great advocate of President Washington, supporting most of his decisions.

After Washington announced he would only serve two terms as president, Adams ran as a Federalist Party candidate against his long-time friend, Thomas Jefferson. Adams received three more electoral votes than Jefferson, making Jefferson his vice president.

Adams served only one term as president from 1797–1801. His presidency was a difficult one. Revolution in France and war in Europe placed the United States between both France and England. Both nations attacked America's merchant ships on the high seas. Such incidents caused Adams to call for the building of a U.S. Navy. Although Adams never asked for war from Congress, the U.S. engaged in an undeclared naval war with France during Adams's presidency.

When Adams sent diplomats to negotiate with the French over the conflict, his representatives were rebuffed and asked to pay a bribe before the French would consider negotiating. Known as the XYZ Affair, Adams had his diplomats recalled.

As pressure mounted at home for the president to declare war on France, Adams took bold steps to rebuild America's confidence and national pride. He expanded the size of American military forces. When political opponents spoke out loudly against Adams, his Federalist Party passed laws designed to limit criticism of the presidency. The Sedition Act made it criminal to criticize the U.S. government and its president. Adams did give limited support to the act.

In the final months of Adams's term, he and Abigail moved into the new White House in Federal City, now Washington, D.C. Then known as the Executive Mansion, the Adamses took up residence in an unfinished home located in the midst of swampy ground. The new capital was small and underpopulated and quite rustic. Only six or so rooms in the Executive Mansion were presentable to the public during the final year of the Adams administration. In fact, Abigail and her servants used the unfinished East Rooms to hang out the family laundry.

When Adams lost his re-election bid in 1800 to Thomas Jefferson, he returned to Quincy where he retired, spending much time writing. John Adams died on July 4, 1826, at age 90.

Review and Write

1. From your reading, what actions taken by Adams reveal that he was a man of integrity and honor?

_____

_____

_____

2. What roles did Adams play during the American Revolution?

_____

_____

_____

3. What challenges did Adams face as president of the United States?

_____

_____

_____

Thomas Jefferson

1801–1809

American Genius

He was a man of extraordinary intellect and talent. His skills, abilities, studies, and interests are impressive—writer, political theorist, musician, philosopher, botanist, farmer, geologist, diplomat, planter, inventor, and educator. Perhaps no other American brought more genius to the presidency than did Thomas Jefferson.

Yet Jefferson remains a man of mysterious dimension. He wrote the words he wished to have carved on his headstone when he died and chose to include only three of his life's accomplishments—author of the Declaration of American Independence, author of the Statute of Virginia for religious freedom, and Father of the University of Virginia. Conspicuously absent from this list was the remarkable fact that he had served his country as its third president.

Other ironies of Jefferson's life include that he was an owner of slaves yet penned the words of the Declaration of Independence which state that all men are created equal. Modern DNA tests suggest that Jefferson fathered a child by a slave woman named Sally Hemmings. Such inconsistencies are troubling. Yet even to his critics, Jefferson remains a powerful symbol of the revolutionary spirit and the principles of democracy.

He was born on April 13, 1743, in Shadwell, Albemarle County, Virginia. His father, Peter Jefferson, was a surveyor, sheriff, and House of Burgesses member. His mother, Jane Randolph Jefferson, came from one of the wealthiest, most aristocratic families in Virginia. Jefferson never considered his aristocratic ties of much importance in determining his identity.

Jefferson's youth was filled with hunting and horseback riding. He fished and canoed on local rivers and streams. Young Tom learned to play the violin and loved music. He shared the family estate with seven siblings, including six sisters.

By age nine he was studying Latin, Greek, and French. Jefferson's father died when Thomas was only 14 years old. Two years later, he entered the College of William and Mary in the colonial capital of Williamsburg. After graduating in two years, he studied law.

In 1769, Jefferson became a member of the Virginia House of Burgesses. Soon afterward, he began building his home—Monticello. This architectural project occupied him on and off for the rest of his life. In 1772, Jefferson married a young widow, Martha Wayles Skelton. While courting, Thomas and Martha played duets together, he on the violin, and she on the harpsichord. Martha bore six children—only two survived into adulthood.

As colonial protests spread in the 1760s and 1770s, Jefferson was an early proponent of the revolution. He wrote a pamphlet in 1774, in which he argued that allegiance to one's monarch was a matter of choice, not command. He helped organize

Jefferson's Monticello

nonimportation agreements against the British to protest taxation.

In 1775, Jefferson was appointed to the Second Continental Congress, which met in Philadelphia. On June 11, he and four other men were selected to write a draft to explain why the Second Continental Congress should vote for independence against Great Britain.

Jefferson and the New United States

Jefferson was soon given the task of writing the Declaration of Independence—one of America's most cherished documents. He wrote that people are born with the same basic rights—life, liberty, and the pursuit of happiness. The declaration was presented to Congress on July 2 and adopted officially on July 4, 1776.

Before year's end, Jefferson returned to Virginia where he served in one of the two new state legislatures of Virginia. In 1779, he proposed a bill for religious freedom. His bill suggested that "all men shall be free to profess . . . their opinions on matters of religion." When the bill passed in 1786, Jefferson considered it one of his greatest achievements. After serving as governor of Virginia for two years, he was elected to the new United States Congress. His efforts in Congress resulted in the adoption of the dollar as the basic monetary unit in the United States. The death of his wife in 1782 was a profound loss for Jefferson.

While Jefferson had accomplished great things

The signing of the Declaration of Independence

well before his 40th birthday, some of his greatest accomplishments lay ahead.

As the new American nation began to develop, Thomas Jefferson always had the growth of the nation in mind. While in Congress, he helped draft the Ordinance of 1784, establishing a process whereby territories could become new states in the Union.

Among his other proposed bills was one which—had it passed— would have outlawed slavery in the western territories by 1800. Although Jefferson owned slaves until his death, he came to believe that institution was evil and should not be allowed to spread.

After 1784, Jefferson lived for the next five years in Europe as a diplomat to France. He was there, watching with interest, when a new constitution was written to govern the young United States. In 1789, he left Paris and returned to America, only to find he had been chosen as President Washington's secretary of state.

While serving in Washington's cabinet, Jefferson came to distrust the politics of another cabinet member, Secretary of State Alexander Hamilton. Hamilton favored a strong federal government that wielded power at the expense of the states. Jefferson preferred a weaker national government, and strong, independent states. Their political differences led to the development of the first political parties in United States history—the Federalists (consisting of Hamilton's followers), and the Democratic-Republicans (who were loyal to Jeffersonian ideals).

When Hamilton appeared to hold more sway over President Washington than Jefferson, he resigned his post late in 1793. Until 1796, Jefferson spent much time at Monticello, experimenting with a new plow, introducing a new variety of peach to American farming, and enjoying his

grandchildren. His country was to call on him again, however.

In 1796, Jefferson was invited to run as the candidate for the Democratic-Republican party after Washington refused to run for a third term. His rival, Federalist John Adams (Washington's vice president) narrowly defeated him. Yet under the political system of the day, Jefferson became Adams's vice president.

Jefferson and the Presidency

After losing the 1796 presidential election to John Adams, Thomas Jefferson found himself serving as Adams's vice president, a role he did not take on with enthusiasm. His chief responsibility was to preside over the Senate, which he did with honor and dignity. Political differences between Adams and Jefferson, however, could not be contained. Jefferson was a Democratic-Republican in a presidential cabinet filled with Federalists. He found support from his party members, which included fellow southerners, as well as northern laborers, and western farmers. As vice president, he was able to strengthen his party. But by 1800, politics had served to nearly destroy the friendship between Jefferson and Adams.

At the end of Adams's term, one disappointing to Jefferson, Jefferson ran for the presidency again, and was elected in 1800. (Jefferson served eight years as president, being re-elected in 1804). His first term was more successful and personally satisfying than his second. During his first term, the United States successfully fought a war with the Barbary pirates of North Africa. He also orchestrated the purchase of the vast Louisiana Territory from the French in 1803 for $15 million, which doubled the size of the United States and its territory at a cost of only 4 cents an acre.

One of his most satisfying endeavors was the

Meriwether Lewis and William Clark

dispatching of Meriwether Lewis and William Clark to explore the vast Louisiana region. Their Corps of Discovery made contact with western Native American tribes, found the source of the Missouri River, and encouraged Americans to move west.

Jefferson's second term was a difficult one. The Napoleonic Wars caused England and France to seize American ships on the high seas and kidnap American sailors. Jefferson countered by encouraging Congress to pass the Embargo Act in December of 1807. This bill prevented all foreign ships from entering American ports, and forbade all American ships from sailing to foreign countries. The results were devastating to American trade. Ships rotted in American harbors, and many Americans were unemployed. It was one of the worse policy moves of the entire Jeffersonian presidency.

In 1809, Jefferson left the presidency and entered his final years of retirement. He and Adams renewed their friendship in 1811, and maintained a warm correspondence for the rest of their lives. Jefferson founded the University of Virginia in 1819. He died on July 4, 1826, the 50th anniversary of the signing of the Declaration of Independence. Without Jefferson's knowledge, his good friend— former President John Adams—died the same day within hours of Jefferson's death.

Review and Write

1. What talents do you think Jefferson used to the greatest extent during his long life?

_____

_____

_____

_____

2. What roles as a patriot did Jefferson play during the American Revolution?

_____

_____

_____

_____

3. Some historians have called Jefferson's attitude toward slavery contradictory. If so, explain how?

_____

_____

_____

_____

James Madison

1809–1817

**James Madison
Father of
the Constitution**

James Madison served his country in a variety of public offices, including the presidency. One of the youngest of the Founding Fathers, Madison made a significant contribution to America's political system by proposing a system of checks and balances for the federal government which developed into the three-branch system—legislative, executive, and judicial—enjoyed by Americans today.

Perhaps more than any other man, Madison deserves to be called the Father of the U.S. Constitution. For his entire life, he was an advocate of republican government. Yet he provided a bridge between Alexander Hamilton's belief in the need for a strong national government at the expense of state power and Jefferson's belief in the primacy of state's rights.

He was born in Virginia, in the home of his maternal grandparents in Port Conway, just a few miles from Fredericksburg. The oldest of 12 children, his parents' families had settled in Virginia during the 1600s. He was a frail and sickly child. Young Madison grew up on a 5000-acre plantation where the family's 100 slaves grew tobacco and field grains. Although Madison personally disliked slavery, he remained an owner of slaves all his life.

Madison was schooled at home, then attended a preparatory school, and later graduated from the College of New Jersey at Princeton. He studied Latin and Greek, and the Enlightenment.

By the 1770s, as the British colonies began loosening England's control, James Madison was beginning a career in politics. In 1774, he served on the Committee of Safety in Orange County, Virginia— a group which provided local government at a time when British authority was being challenged. In 1776, he helped author a new Virginia state constitution. Later that year, he served as a member of Virginia's first state legislature where he met Thomas Jefferson. The two became lifelong friends.

Madison served on the governor's council in 1777 during the Revolutionary War, and worked closely with two governors—Patrick Henry and Thomas Jefferson. He later represented his home state for nearly four years in the Continental Congress, beginning in 1780.

Madison continued his political involvement when the American Revolution ended in 1783. He promoted a strong national government, yet the country's first constitution—the Articles of Confederation—created a weak government. In just a few years, opposition to the Articles led to the Constitutional Convention in Philadelphia.

He was present at the meetings of the Constitutional Convention during the summer of

1787. Madison prepared for the convention by buying 200 books on government, political policy, democracy, and history. By summer's end, a new constitution was complete. That document clearly bore the imprint of Madison's political ideals of government by the people.

The Presidency of James Madison

Over the next thirty years, Madison was actively involved in national public office. He served four terms in the House of Representatives from 1789 to 1797. During those years, he married a widow named Dolly Payne Todd.

After a few years of retirement to his Virginia plantation, he was appointed by President Jefferson as his secretary of state. His eight-year tenure led to his candidacy for president in 1808. He won that election against Federalist candidate C. C. Pinckney.

Within his first term, Madison soon felt pressure to go to war against Great Britain. The British naval practice of impressment of American sailors led him to go to war in the summer of 1812. Congress approved the president's request for a declaration of war on June 18, 1812. (Five months later, the American people showed their support for Madison by electing him to a second term.)

Even as war developed, Madison knew that the young United States was ill-prepared for military conflict with Great Britain—the greatest naval power on earth. He understood that the war would be difficult to win and that American trade would be greatly disrupted. But he also understood that most Americans were tired of being insulted and bullied.

The War of 1812 proved a difficult one. British ships blockaded American ports, and early military campaigns against British-held Canada were failures. The war's low point came when British troops marched into the American capital, and burned the Capitol building, the White House, and other government buildings. (Mrs. Madison barely escaped from the White House ahead of British troops, and the president spent part of one night hiding in a hen house.)

During the days that followed, the British assault on nearby Fort McHenry failed. (During that attack, lawyer Francis Scott Key wrote the poem *The Star-Spangled Banner*.) As the war dragged on, the British lost their determination and negotiated the war's conclusion in December 1814.

With the war's conclusion, the United States was able to expand its international trade without threat from Great Britain. Although the war had been difficult, Americans emerged from Mr. Madison's war with a renewed sense of national pride. Madison's secretary of the treasury, Albert Gallatin, noted, "people . . . are more American; they feel and act more as a nation."

As president, Madison pursued a varied agenda. He supported a recharter of the National Bank, tariffs to protect U.S. industry, and a federal program of road and canal construction. One such highway, the National or Cumberland Road, was begun in 1811.

In retirement, Madison worked on Montpelier—his estate in Virginia. After 1826 and the death of Thomas Jefferson, he served as rector (president) of the University of Virginia. Madison also served his native state as a member of the Virginia Constitutional Convention of 1829. He died in 1836.

Review and Write

1. Why is James Madison qualified to be called the Father of the Constitution?

_____

_____

_____

2. What did the successful end of the War of 1812 bring to the young United States?

_____

_____

_____

_____

James Monroe

1817–1825

From Patriot to Politician

Those who knew him saw James Monroe as a practical man. He was not a quick thinker, a deep philosopher, a fiery speaker, or a skilled writer. Yet he brought to politics an open, able, and ready mind. He pursued his goals with honesty, thoughtfulness, and personal warmth, and found he could persuade those around him with the power of his charm and character.

Such qualities reminded some people of George Washington. Monroe's career in public service was as lengthy as Washington's, comprising 40 years of fighting during the Revolution, elections to office, and serving as diplomat to Great Britain, France, and Spain. As president, he gave direction to a nation that was growing, expanding, and moving west.

James Monroe was born in Virginia on April 28, 1758. The oldest of five children, his father's family had lived in Virginia for generations. As a youth, he went to school at the home of a neighbor, walking to his studies. He often took along a rifle, shooting wild game as he made his way through the Virginia forest.

Although he entered the College of William and Mary in 1774 at age 16, the American Revolution distracted him. When only 18, Monroe enlisted in the army. He fought at Brandywine, Germantown, and Monmouth, and was wounded at Trenton.

Young Monroe witnessed the hardships of the Valley Forge encampment during the winter of 1778.

During the war, Monroe was promoted to the rank of lieutenant colonel. Following the Valley Forge winter, Monroe was ordered to return to his native Virginia to help increase enlistments from his home state. He did not enjoy the task and did not succeed greatly at it. While in Virginia, however, he met the governor of the state, Thomas Jefferson. By then a famous patriotic leader, Jefferson struck up an acquaintance with young Monroe—one which developed into a lifelong friendship.

By 1780, Monroe left the military and studied law and political theory under the tutelage of his old friend, Thomas Jefferson. Two years later, he was elected to the Virginia House and later served in the Congress of the Confederation until 1786. Before year's end, Monroe married 17-year-old Elizabeth Kortright, a strikingly beautiful young woman. During their marriage, they had three children.

The next year, Monroe joined with his friend James Madison in support of the writing of a new constitution. However, he came to oppose the ratification of that document, believing it granted too much power to the Senate. When ratification took place, Monroe accepted it.

Over the following years, Monroe worked closely on political issues with James Madison and Thomas Jefferson. Between them, they organized the

Democratic-Republican Party and declared the agenda of the Federalist Party.

The 1790s found Monroe ever involved in the growth of the young United States. He served as minister to France beginning in 1794 and as governor of Virginia from 1799 to 1802.

The Presidency of James Monroe

In 1803, his diplomacy with the French led to the American purchase of the vast Louisiana Territory. This bit of land dealing made Monroe a prominent, national figure, one destined for the presidency.

His role in negotiating the Louisiana Purchase led President Jefferson to enlist Monroe's skills in negotiating with Spain for American annexation of Florida. Working in Madrid with another American negotiator, Charles Pinckney, Monroe's efforts failed. Yet recognizing him as a skilled diplomat, Jefferson appointed Monroe as minister to Great Britain, a post he held until 1807.

Finally, in 1808, Monroe ran for the presidency against his old friend Madison, who won the nomination and the election. In 1811, Madison appointed Monroe his secretary of state. War with Britain broke out in 1812. After the British burning of Washington, D. C., Madison replaced his secretary of war with Monroe.

Monroe's national presence made him an obvious candidate for the presidency in 1816—a race he won over Federalist candidate Rufus King of New York. As president, Monroe witnessed the collapse of the Federalist Party. Without the clash of two political parties, the times were called the Era of Good Feelings.

Despite a depression from 1818 to 1819, the Monroe years were prosperous in America. When the speaker of the house, Henry Clay, of Kentucky promoted his American System to encourage American growth through federally sponsored road and canal construction, and protective tariffs for domestic industry, Monroe did not offer his support. He felt Congress did not have the authority to build roads and canals.

Much of Monroe's success as president lay in his

foreign policy. Treaties formed with Great Britain, and Spain opened up western lands for American settlement. Such victories secured Monroe's election to a second term in 1820. During his second term, Monroe issued his foreign policy doctrine which closed the Americas to any further colonization by Europe.

Monroe left the presidency in 1825 and served as regent of the University of Virginia until 1829. He died in 1831, his public service having reduced him to poverty.

Review and Write

1. How did James Monroe remind people of George Washington?

2. What role did Monroe have in expanding the size of the United States and its territory?

3. In what area did Monroe achieve his greatest success as president? How?

John Quincy Adams

1825–1829

The Second Adams

The sixth president of the United States, John Quincy Adams, was not new to the White House when he took office. His father, President John Adams, had lived there during the final months of his term in office. These two men—father and son—shared other similarities. Both served a single term as president. They were both highly intellectual and well educated. They had trouble in social encounters with anyone other than close friends. And they both felt strongly about the United States and the great republic's future.

John Quincy's political career, while not as full and varied as his father's, was nevertheless personally rewarding. And after leaving the presidency, he went on to pursue another political career as a member of the House of Representatives. There, he became an active and vocal opponent of American slavery until his death.

He was born on July 11, 1767, in Braintree, Massachusetts, just as his father had been. While a young man during the American Revolution, John Quincy received home schooling from his mother, Abigail. He followed his father on diplomatic missions to Europe, where he was schooled at a private Parisian academy and at the University of Leyden. While only in his teens, he traveled as an interpreter for the first American diplomat to Russia. Upon returning to America, he studied at Harvard and graduated in 1787. He took up the practice of law in 1790 in Boston.

In 1794, President Washington appointed John Quincy minister to the Netherlands. While in Europe, he met and courted his future wife, Louisa Catherine Johnson. They married in 1797.

When John Adams became president the same year, he appointed his son minister to Prussia. During these years, the John Quincy Adamses gave birth to four children. They named their firstborn George Washington Adams. Their youngest son, Charles Francis, served as minister to England.

John Quincy was recalled from Prussia by his father when Thomas Jefferson was elected president in 1800. In just a few years, John Quincy was elected to the Massachusetts Senate (1802) and then to the U.S. Senate the following year. Adams's independent-mindedness caused him to frequently vote alongside the Democratic-Republicans, although he was officially a Federalist.

When Congress supported President Jefferson's Embargo Act of 1807, John Quincy Adams bolted the Federalist Party and supported the Democratic-Republican measure. This cost him his Senate seat in 1808. With that loss, John Quincy decided to quit politics and become a Harvard professor of oratory and rhetoric. But he did not stay out of public life long.

In 1809, President James Madison appointed Adams as minister to Russia, then to Great Britain. In 1815, he helped negotiate the Treaty of Ghent which ended the War of 1812. In 1817, President James Monroe named him secretary of state. His treaties with Spain gave America control of Florida and ended Spanish claim to the Oregon Country. He helped Monroe hammer out his Monroe Doctrine.

The Presidency of John Quincy Adams

His political successes made Adams a serious contender for the presidency in 1824. The race proved a difficult one, with five candidates crowding the field, including the hero of the War of 1812, Andrew Jackson, and Henry Clay from Kentucky. It was a mud-slinging campaign, with Adams's supporters claiming Jackson unfit for the presidency, accusing him of having a wife who was already married to another man. Jackson's men were equally ruthless. Adams was accused of providing prostitutes for the tsar while the diplomat was minister to Russia.

Jackson proved to be Adams's strongest opponent. One slogan of the day seemed to tell the story for both sides: "John Quincy Adams who can write; Andrew Jackson who can fight!" Adams prevailed, but only when the election was thrown into the House of Representatives, since no candidate carried a majority vote.

As president, Adams called for a powerful Bank of the United States, a national tariff protecting domestic industry, the expansion of national lands, and internal improvements, such as roads, canals, and a new means of transportation—railroads. He called for the establishment of a national university and a national observatory. Congress agreed to neither.

Not a popular president, Adams once again faced a challenge in the election of 1828 from Andrew Jackson. In fact, Adams's own vice president, John C. Calhoun of South Carolina, ran against Adams, choosing to run as Jackson's vice-presidential running mate. Adams did not actively campaign. He lost the electoral vote 178 to 83.

Although he intended to retire, when his neighbors in Quincy encouraged him to run for the House of Representatives, he agreed, and was elected in 1830. He served in the House for the next 17 years.

Adams's early terms in the House coincided with Jackson's presidency. As might be expected, he fought Jackson's opposition to the second Bank of the United States and the president's support of statehood for Texas.

Several times, Adams attempted to introduce antislavery legislation. But such talk was not popular in the Congress among southern representatives. In 1836, the House voted to adopt several resolutions called *Gag Rules* which prohibited even discussing the limiting of slavery in any way. Adams strongly opposed such measures and was instrumental in getting them repealed in 1844.

On February 21, 1848, Adams suffered a stroke at his desk in the House chamber. Too weak to move, he died two days later in the Speaker's room. He was buried in the Unitarian Church cemetery in Quincy.

Review and Write

1. List some of the similarities between John Quincy Adams and his famous father, John Adams.

_____

_____

2. From your reading here, in what ways did John Quincy Adams prove himself a man of principle?

_____

_____

3. The three presidents prior to John Quincy Adams were all slave-holding southerners. How was he different?

_____

_____

Andrew Jackson

1829–1837

Man of the People

Until Andrew Jackson became the seventh president in 1829, America's chief executives (except for the Adamses of Massachusetts) hailed from prominent, if not wealthy, Virginia planter families. Presidents from Washington to John Quincy Adams were well educated and well-bred, having risen from the ranks of the social upper class.

Not so with Andrew Jackson who was the first president born in a log cabin. Raised on the frontier and orphaned at 14, Jackson became a national figure through his military leadership during the War of 1812, and as an Indian fighter. Although not born to money and prestige, Jackson attained respectability through hard work and determination.

He lived during a time in American history when the United States was moving into its second generation and shifting away from the so-called Virginia Dynasty—from presidents who seemed too upper-class, too far removed from the lives of the average American. Jackson came to symbolize the Common Man.

Average Americans were gaining access to the political process. The new American democracy allowed more white males to vote than ever before. Political reforms such as the secret ballot became more commonplace.

Jackson was the first president to be nominated by a national convention of the people. It is not surprising that Jackson appealed to such an electorate of voters, given his common roots and his often rough approach to American politics.

Born on the eve of the American Revolutionary period, on March 15, 1767, Jackson was a child of the Carolina frontier. His parents had only arrived in America two years earlier. They were poor farmers. Andrew's father died just days after his son's birth leaving him to make his own way in the world.

Growing up, Andrew was a tough young man. He was prone to fights and would never surrender to a stronger opponent. His lifelong stubborn nature was evident even in his early years. Although he sporadically attended boarding school, he was much more interested in cockfighting and outdoor activities.

In 1780, when only 13 years old, Jackson and his brother Robert joined a colonial militia unit. When both young men were captured by the British the following year, he challenged one of his captors by refusing to shine the officer's boots. The soldier struck Jackson with his sword, leaving a saber scar on the young man's head, which he carried for life.

Although their mother was able to gain her sons' release, both Robert and Mrs. Jackson soon died of smallpox, leaving Andrew alone.

By war's end, Jackson turned to the study of

law. Much to his surprise, he inherited 300 pounds from a long forgotten uncle in Ireland—a significant amount in that day. While Jackson might have used this money to establish himself as a landowner, instead he wasted his inheritance on gambling. Such behavior gave no hint that Jackson would one day be a leader of armies and hold the highest office in the land.

A Man of the Frontier

Despite some youthful indiscretions, Andrew Jackson returned to his law studies and was admitted to the bar at age 20. (The standard for lawyers on the frontier was not strict.) He moved west and took a position in Nashville, Tennessee, as a public prosecutor. There he speculated in land and slaves. He was known to have purchased land for only 10 cents an acre and later sold it for $3 an acre. In 1788, he met and fell in love with Rachel Donelson Robards. Since she was already married—to a violent and jealous captain—Andrew did not pursue a relationship until he believed she had obtained a legal divorce.

Andrew married Rachel in Natchez, Mississippi, in August 1791. Two years later, the couple was startled to discover that Rachel's husband had not actually obtained a divorce in Virginia as she had been led to believe. When the divorce was actually completed in September of 1793, the Jacksons were married again in early 1794 in Nashville. This awkward and embarrassing chapter in the lives of the Jacksons would later be used against Andrew when he ran for the presidency in 1828.

But first Jackson had to make a name for himself. Ahead of him lay years of politics and military service and a role in the War of 1812 that would catapult him to national prominence.

Despite the awkward beginning for the Jackson marriage, their relationship was a happy and loving one. Although they never had any children of their own, they adopted four of Rachel's nephews between 1809 and 1819.

Just two years following the Jacksons' remarriage, Andrew was elected to the U.S. House of Representatives in 1796. Jackson had served as a delegate to the convention which created the state constitution for the new state of Tennessee—the first added to the young nation after the original 13 states. Jackson may have proposed the name of Tennessee for the new western state. In 1797, the

Andrew Jackson's plantation home, "The Hermitage"

Tennessee legislature appointed Jackson to the U.S. Senate. This was not a role he enjoyed.

He did not like life in Philadelphia (the American capital at that time) and had pressures in his personal life. Thus, he resigned from the Senate in 1798. Before year's end, however, he was back in Tennessee politics where he gained a position on the state's supreme court in September. He held that position for the next six years.

In 1804, Jackson resigned from the court and returned to private life. Although he attempted to run two plantations during his judgeship, his many debts forced him to sell one of them. From then on he focused on the other estate, known as the Hermitage. He also became co-owner in a general store and a nearby stable where he kept racehorses. His financial state improved from the winnings of his racehorses at the track.

From time to time, Jackson's fiery temper led him to participate in duels. In 1806, he killed a lawyer named Charles Dickinson. Jackson was seriously wounded himself and carried a pistol ball in one of his lungs for the rest of his life.

The Rise of Andrew Jackson

As a westerner, Andrew Jackson was jubilant when the War of 1812 erupted and England and America were enemies once again. Although he had been critical of President Madison's slowness in taking the British to task for their seizure of American ships and the impressment of U.S. sailors, Jackson offered his military services to Madison at the war's outset.

A commission did not come from Madison, however, and Jackson was forced to settle for a commission as major general of U.S. volunteers. Jackson was sent to Natchez, Mississippi, but before he and his men saw action, they were ordered to disband. Jackson was furious. He marched his men back to Tennessee. It was on this campaign that Andrew Jackson—a tough military commander—gained the nickname of Old Hickory.

But Jackson's military efforts were not over. He next took command of 2000 men in a campaign against the Creek Indians, who had murdered

several hundred pioneers at Fort Mims in modern-day Alabama. He defeated the Creek at Horseshoe Bend on March 27, 1814. Under the terms of the peace treaty, the Creek surrendered 23,000,000 acres of land.

With this success, the U.S. Army commissioned Jackson as a major general. He was ordered to move to the vicinity of New Orleans, where a British landing was expected. With a force of 5000 men, an army which included regular U.S. Army troops, volunteers from Kentucky and Tennessee, free blacks from New Orleans, and even the famous pirate Jean Laffite and his crew, Jackson met the British on January 8, 1815. Although outnumbered by 8000 British forces, Jackson won the day—his opponents suffering nearly 2000 casualties. Jackson's army only tallied about 70 casualties.

General Jackson's victory at New Orleans catapulted him to national prominence. After an abortive campaign against the Seminole Indians in Florida, Jackson finally resigned from military service in 1821. In 1823, he was re-elected to the U.S. Senate.

The following year, the Tennessee legislature nominated Jackson for the presidency. The 1824 presidential race featured four Democratic-Republican Party members—Jackson, Henry Clay, John Quincy Adams, and William Crawford. When the electoral votes were counted, Jackson polled 99 votes; Adams 84; and the other two combined, 78. Yet Jackson soon discovered that he had not yet won the election.

Despite Jackson's greater vote total during the 1824 presidential election, he did not win the election. His 99 votes did not constitute a majority, so the election was decided in the House of Representatives according to the U.S. Constitution. Once in the House, Henry Clay dropped out of the race and gave his support (and his 37 electoral votes) to Adams, which made Adams the victor.

Jackson and his supporters were furious. He accused Adams and Clay of having made a corrupt bargain. (Clay was later appointed by Adams as his secretary of state.) For the next four years, Jackson's supporters caused Adams many problems and embarrassment. While Jackson resigned from the Senate in 1825, he set his sights on the 1828 election.

The Presidency of Andrew Jackson

The 1828 presidential campaign pitted Jackson against President Adams. It proved to be one of the dirtiest in American history. Both sides accused the other's candidate of unscrupulous activity. Adams's men accused Jackson of adultery for having lived with Rachel while she was still married. Jackson's supporters accused Adams of providing prostitutes for the tsar of Russia and of buying billiard tables for the White House with government monies. The campaign avoided the issues, and people tended to vote on the personalities of the two candidates. Jackson defeated President Adams with 178 to 83 electoral votes.

Jackson's election joy was cut short, however, when his wife Rachel died the following month from a heart attack. He blamed her death on the viciousness of the election campaign. She was buried at the Hermitage. Jackson became a bitter man. "May God Almighty forgive her murderers as I know she forgave them," said Jackson. "I never can."

When he took office in March 1829, the capital was crowded with Jackson's well-wishers. They were common people—frontiersmen, westerners, and farmers—who crowded into the White House during the reception and left it in a shambles. The era of the Common Man in American politics had begun.

Jackson's first administration introduced the spoils system to American politics. He replaced 2000 federal appointees with his supporters, touching off controversy. Further controversy racked his cabinet as clashes, both personal and political, developed between Jackson and Vice President John C. Calhoun of South Carolina. When some cabinet members sided with Calhoun on the issues, Jackson replaced them.

The Bank of the United States proved to be the significant political controversy of Jackson's first term. Jackson felt the bank was unconstitutional. When a bill came before him to recharter it in 1832, he vetoed it. Without the bank's financial stability, the stage was set for an economic depression, which came in 1837.

Jackson ran for re-election in 1832. That year,

significant changes took place in American politics. For the first time, the candidates were chosen at national nominating conventions. Jackson was opposed by Henry Clay, who broke from his party and ran as a National Republican. Jackson won a decisive victory over Clay.

Serious clashes over high tariffs caused Vice President Calhoun to resign his office, and his home state threatened to strike down or nullify any new tariff bill. Jackson moved forcefully during this nullification crisis, threatening military action against South Carolina. Henry Clay managed to defuse the crisis by introducing a Compromise Tariff bill in the House in 1833. The nullification crisis only managed to drive Calhoun and Jackson further apart.

Controversy and land questions led to a crisis for the Cherokee Indians during Jackson's second term. Georgians threatened to seize Cherokee land, and the Cherokee took their cause to court. Although they won their case, Jackson ordered their removal to land west of the Mississippi River. By the end of Jackson's second term, nearly all Native Americans living east of the Mississippi had been removed to west of the Mississippi.

Jackson left the presidency in 1837 tired and sick, his hair white, and his lungs tubercular. He spent his final days at the Hermitage, riding horseback almost daily, and keeping a keen eye on the direction of American politics. In the summer of 1845, Jackson died and was later buried at the Hermitage next to his wife, Rachel.

Review and Write

How important were Jackson's exploits in establishing him as a national figure and a presidential candidate?

_____

_____

_____

_____

_____

Test I

Part I.

Multiple Choice.
Match the information at the left to the answers on the right. Place the letter of the correct answer in the spaces below.

1. Traditionally, this government official swears in incoming presidents.
2. Wrote the Declaration of Independence.
3. President who declared America's neutrality during the French Revolution.
4. Married a young widow who had inherited 17,000 acres and over $300,000.
5. As president, his agents negotiated the purchase of the Louisiana Territory.
6. Congress passed the Embargo Act during his presidency.
7. As a young man, he helped survey the property of Lord Fairfax.
8. Lawyer who defended the British soldiers involved in the Boston Massacre.
9. The XYZ Affair occurred during his presidency.
10. This Amendment limits the number of years someone may serve as president.
11. Was accused of assassinating a French ambassador in the Ohio Country.
12. The only American president to not belong to a political party.

A. George Washington
B. Thomas Jefferson
C. Chief Justice
D. 23rd Amendment
E. 22nd Amendment
F. 20th Amendment
G. Speaker of the House
H. John Adams

Answers:

1. ____ 2. ____ 3. ____ 4. ____ 5. ____ 6. ____ 7. ____ 8. ____ 9. ____ 10. ____ 11. ____ 12. ____

Part II.

Multiple Choice.
Match the information at the left to the answers on the right. Place the letter of the correct answer in the spaces below.

1. Construction of the National Road was begun during his presidency.
2. Defeated the British at the battle of New Orleans.
3. As secretary of state, he negotiated U.S. control of Florida from Spain.
4. Once killed a man during a duel.
5. Is often referred to as the Father of the U.S. Constitution.
6. Defeated Creek Indians at the battle of Horseshoe Bend.
7. He was born poor on the Carolina frontier.
8. His executive policy closed the Americas to further European colonization.
9. Was wounded during the Revolutionary War battle at Trenton.
10. Introduced the spoils system to American politics.
11. Was slashed by a British officer's sword during the Revolutionary War.
12. As president, he called for the establishment of a national university.

A. Andrew Jackson
B. James Monroe
C. John Quincy Adams
D. James Madison

Answers:

1. ____ 2. ____ 3. ____ 4. ____ 5. ____ 6. ____ 7. ____ 8. ____ 9. ____ 10. ____ 11. ____ 12. ____

Martin Van Buren

1837–1841

The Rise of Martin Van Buren

The eighth president of the United States, Martin Van Buren, was born at the end of the American Revolution. His rise to the presidency marks the second generation of America's executive leadership.

As Andrew Jackson's first secretary of state and second vice president (following the resignation of John C. Calhoun in 1833), Van Buren became one of Jackson's loyalist supporters, ensuring his nomination for the presidency in 1836. He was a man of conviction, just as Andrew Jackson had been, and he believed in a prosperous and growing America, while advocating the belief that the less government interferes, the better for general prosperity.

Such convictions did not serve him or the United States well in 1837, when America slipped into the first of its great economic depressions. As the country slid into financial ruin, Van Buren did little to stop it.

Martin Van Buren was born in the old Dutch town of Kinderhook, New York, on December 5, 1782. He was the middle child of five born to Abraham and Maria Hoes Van Buren. His father was a tavern keeper and small-time farmer. His mother, a widower, brought three additional children to the Van Buren marriage. Young Martin attended the local village school and grew up hearing his Dutch neighbors argue politics in his father's drinking establishment.

By age 14, Martin was studying law under a local lawyer. By 1803, he was admitted to the bar and took up law practice in his hometown. Four years later he married a distant cousin, Hannah Hoes. They had four sons, one of whom later became presidential secretary to his father. Mrs. Van Buren died several years before Martin became president.

A proponent of Thomas Jefferson, Van Buren became a Democratic-Republican and was elected to the New York senate in 1812. He became the state attorney general four years later and held the office until 1819, when a new state governor removed him for political reasons.

In 1821, Martin Van Buren was elected to the U.S. Senate. From the Senate floor, Van Buren spoke out against American slave trade and led a reform effort to abolish debtor's prison. He was popular back home in New York and was re-elected in 1827. During these years, Van Buren became a proponent of presidential candidate, Andrew Jackson.

Following Jackson's election in 1828, he appointed Martin Van Buren as his secretary of state. Van Buren worked on improving U.S. and British relations, and negotiated the reopening of British West Indian ports to American merchant shipping. In 1831, Jackson nominated Van Buren for U.S. minister to Great Britain, but his enemies in the Senate voted him down by one vote. The next year, when Vice President John C. Calhoun resigned, Jackson appointed Martin as his replacement.

The Presidency of Martin Van Buren

As vice president, Van Buren was a clear supporter of Jackson and his policies, even those which helped destroy the Bank of the United States. While presiding over the Senate, such issues caused Van Buren's enemies to view him with animosity. Rumors circulated of a plot to kill Van Buren. The vice president took such tales seriously enough to arm himself with a pistol while on the Senate floor.

Van Buren's loyal support of Jackson led to his becoming the presidential candidate in 1836. He won that election over Whig Party candidate, William Henry Harrison, of Indiana. Neither of the two men running for the vice-presidency won a majority of the electoral votes. For the first and only time in American history, the Senate chose the vice president, logically selecting Van Buren's running mate, Richard M. Johnson, of Kentucky.

Almost immediately after taking office, problems for Van Buren began. The country slipped into an economic depression called the Panic of 1837. It was the first great depression of the 1800s. Van Buren's political philosophy caused him to do little to battle the depression. Businesses floundered and banks closed as unemployment rose.

Van Buren's only response to the depression was the withdrawal of federal deposits from private banks. He placed those monies in a federal treasury.

Other problems worked against the Van Buren presidency. Border disputes with Canada led to armed conflict. A war with the Seminole Indians in Florida proved costly and ineffective. When Van Buren appeared to move slowly on the annexation of Texas, pro-slavery advocates criticized Van Buren.

When Van Buren campaigned for re-election in 1840, he found himself running against his challenger of 1836, the old Indian fighter and former governor of Indiana, William Henry Harrison. Harrison's supporters ran their candidate with great enthusiasm, while the Democratic party was badly divided.

The Democrats refused to give their support to the re-election of Vice President Johnson, so Van Buren ran for re-election without a vice-presidential running mate. The Whigs ran a strong, exuberant campaign, complete with music, banners, parades, hard cider, and slogans such as "Tippecanoe and Tyler, too." (The slogan referred to Harrison's earlier victory over Indians at the Battle of Tippecanoe.) Van Buren lost the election to Harrison.

Van Buren never held public office again, but he remained involved in politics. He ran for the presidency in 1848 on an antislavery platform, but lost. He survived to see the coming of the Civil War, and died in the summer of 1862.

Review and Write

1. What was Van Buren's philosophy of government?

_____

_____

_____

2. How did he use this philosophy in response to the Panic of 1837?

_____

_____

_____

3. In what ways did Van Buren serve the Jackson administration?

_____

_____

_____

_____

William Henry Harrison

1841

Although William Henry Harrison had a rich and varied life as territorial governor of Indiana, soldier, U.S. senator, and diplomat, he is perhaps most remembered most for the shortness of his presidency —a mere 30 days.

Born in Charles City County, Virginia, on February 9, 1773, William Harrison was the youngest of seven children. His father, Benjamin Harrison, served in the Continental Congress during the Revolutionary War and signed the Declaration of Independence.

Harrison attended the University of Pennsylvania, studying medicine. When his father died in 1791, Harrison left college and joined the military. He fought in the Northwest Territory against the Indians at the Battle of Fallen Timbers in 1794.

In 1795, Harrison married Anna Symmes. Their 19-year marriage produced ten children. Harrison resigned his commission in 1798, and President Adams appointed him secretary of the Northwest Territory. Two years later, he was named governor of the Indiana Territory, an office he held until 1812.

Harrison was protective of the Native Americans in the region, seeing that they were inoculated against smallpox. However, when he negotiated a treaty transferring tribal land to white settlement, the Shawnee rallied under their leader, Tecumseh. Harrison engaged the Shawnee in the Battle of Tippecanoe on November 7, 1811.

After a successful campaign against the British during the War of 1812, Harrison returned to politics, and was elected to the House of Representatives in 1816. He was selected for the U.S. Senate in 1825. He briefly served as U.S. minister to Colombia.

In 1836, Harrison ran for the presidency as a Whig (a party formed to oppose Andrew Jackson) and lost against Van Buren. Harrison ran again in 1840. Harrison himself did not campaign. In fact, he was ordered by the leaders of the Whig Party to speak not a word about his principles or creed. Instead of running on the issues, the Whigs campaigned for him with parades and slogans ("Tippecanoe and Tyler, too!") and claimed their candidate was born in a log cabin—a false claim.

Such claims were designed to appeal to the common man, those who had given their support to Andrew Jackson for president just eight years earlier. This time, Harrison won the election.

When Harrison took office, it was raining on Inauguration Day. He caught a cold—which developed into pneumonia—and died on April 4, 1841, the 31st day of his presidency.

Review and Write

Which do you believe may have played a greater role in Harrison's rise to the presidency— his military background or his work in politics and diplomacy?

John Tyler

1841–1845

John Tyler was the first vice president to become the chief executive following a president's death. He left the Democrats to run with Harrison, who was a Whig. As president, he faced political isolation, and was accepted by neither the Whigs nor the Democrats.

Politically, he was a conservative, as were many presidents of this era. He believed in a small federal government that did not interfere in the lives of citizens. He advocated a view of republicanism akin to Thomas Jefferson.

Born to a Virginia governor in Charles City County (Harrison's home county) on March 29, 1790, Tyler attended the College of William and Mary at age 12. He studied law and was admitted to the bar at 19.

Over the next 30 years, Tyler served as a member of the Virginia House of Delegates, fought in the War of 1812, and was elected to the U.S. House of Representatives. He was chancellor of William and Mary College and governor of Virginia from 1825 to 1827. In that year, he was elected to the U.S. Senate.

As a strict interpreter of the U.S. Constitution, Tyler was disappointed in the politics of President Jackson. In 1836, when the Virginia legislature ordered Tyler to support Jackson, who was facing a censure vote by the Senate, he refused and resigned his office. In 1840, the Whigs chose him to run as Harrison's vice-presidential running mate to gain southern votes. He agreed to run as a Whig candidate when he thought the Whigs no longer supported restoration of the Bank of the United States, and legislation in support of higher tariffs.

He and Harrison won, and Tyler was soon catapulted to the White House following Harrison's death after only a month in office. Some politicians did not respect him as president. As the first man to inherit the presidency, he had to convince others of his legitimacy. His critics were ruthless, referring to him as His Accidency.

As president, Tyler struggled with opposition from the Whigs. When they supported a national bank and new tariffs, Tyler vetoed their efforts in Congress. Whigs even supported mobs to surround the White House to intimidate Tyler. But he stood firm.

The Whigs introduced impeachment resolutions against him in 1843, which were later dropped. He brought an end to the Seminole War in Florida, witnessed the annexation of Texas as a state, admitted Florida, and signed the Pre-Emption Act, which granted 160 acres to any settler who built a cabin on his property. Following his presidency, Tyler retired to his plantation in Virginia where he died on January 18, 1862. He had just been elected to the Confederate House of Representatives.

Review and Write

Although the Whigs chose Tyler as their vice-presidential candidate, what factors brought about a split between him and his adopted party?

James K. Polk
1845–1849

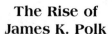

The Rise of James K. Polk

Few presidents have enjoyed a presidency as successful as that of James K. Polk, who served one term between 1845 and 1849. The U.S. added more territory during his presidency than at any other time. Land that today includes nine states became American territory while Polk presided over the nation. Three new states were added to the Union—Texas (1845), Iowa (1846), and Wisconsin (1848).

Unlike most presidents, Polk accomplished all the goals he set for himself and the nation. The 1840s was an exciting decade which witnessed the California gold rush, the invention of the telegraph, and the mass migration of thousands of pioneers along the western Oregon Trail. Polk successfully guided the United States through a war with Mexico.

However, Polk's personality did not make him popular with the American people. He was a cold, aggressive, and uncompromising man. Driven by his own ambition, Polk emerged from his single term as president exhausted. His health broken, he did not live more than three months after the end of his presidency.

As with Andrew Jackson before him, James K. Polk was born in Carolina country on November 2, 1795, the oldest of ten children. His parents were Samuel Polk and Jane Knox Polk who had migrated to America from Ireland. The name *Polk* was taken from the old family name of "Pollock" or "Pollok." At age 11, Polk moved with his family to Tennessee, which he called his home for the remainder of his life. He later attended the University of North Carolina, graduating at the top of his class. He studied law and was admitted to the bar in 1820, practicing law in Tennessee.

Working within the Democratic Party, Polk became clerk of the Tennessee Senate and was elected to the House in 1823. He supported Jackson, a fellow Tennessean, for the presidency. Jackson took notice of young Polk and followed his career in politics during later years. (Polk was sometimes called Young Hickory, as a tribute to Jackson's Old Hickory.)

In 1824, Polk married Sarah Childress on New Year's Day. She was a dark-eyed, black-haired woman. A strict Moravian, Sarah was highly religious. As First Lady, she banned alcohol, dancing, and card-playing from the White House. She and President Polk refused to attend horseraces and the theater, considering both to be immoral. Sarah was a strong supporter of her husband and served as his presidential secretary. He called her by the name Sally.

In 1825, Polk's political career turned national when he was elected to the first of seven consecutive terms in the U.S. House of Representatives. As a loyal Jackson supporter and Democrat, Polk opposed the policies of President John Quincy Adams. Through 14 years in the House, Polk was tireless, absent from congressional sessions on only one occasion.

In 1839, Jackson convinced Polk to run for the governorship of Tennessee. As governor, Polk continued to work hard. He supported slavery, states' rights, and limited power for the federal government. Although he put himself tirelessly into his role as governor, he was not re-elected in 1841.

The Fabulous 40s

During the 1844 Democratic convention, Polk soon found himself the candidate for the presidency. When the convention opened, Polk was not a serious contender for the nomination. President Van Buren anticipated being renominated. But Van Buren had lost Democratic support in the West and South when he held up annexation of Texas to the Union. Polk spoke out in favor of Texas's admission and the annexation of the Oregon Country as well. These positions helped Polk win the nomination over Van Buren and others.

The 1844 election pitted Polk against Whig candidate Henry Clay of Kentucky. Despite the fact that many in America did not know who Polk was before the campaign, he was elected by a majority of 40,000 votes. As president, Polk continued to tirelessly achieve his four chief political goals—to lower tariff rates, reestablish the independent treasury, establish the boundary of Oregon with Great Britain, and gain California for the Union.

The Oregon boundary was achieved through the Oregon Treaty of 1846. The same year, a Polk-sponsored tariff was introduced in Congress and passed. Polk pushed the Independent Treasury Act through Congress also in 1846. The acquisition of California proved to be more difficult for Polk.

After failing to buy California from the Mexican government, Polk provoked a war with Mexico over the boundary between Mexico and Texas. When Polk ordered American troops south of the Nueces River in Texas, the Mexicans attacked on April 25, 1846. After two years of fighting, a defeated Mexico signed away all claims to Texas and granted land to the United States, which included California and the southwest region.

From the lands gained from Mexico after the war, the United States gained control over territory which would later include not only California, but Arizona, Colorado, Nevada, New Mexico, Utah, and Wyoming.

In 1848, his goals achieved, Polk refused to run for the presidency again. (He was the first president to choose not to run for a second term.) He left the presidency in 1849, his four years in the White House having proven exhausting. He returned to his land in his home state of Tennessee where he died just months later of a bout of cholera.

Review and Write

1. How important was the West to Polk and to his presidency?

_____

_____

_____

2. When Mexico refused to sell California to the U.S., what did Polk do to gain California?

_____

_____

_____

_____

3. Would you consider Polk's presidency a success? Explain.

_____

_____

_____

_____

_____

Zachary Taylor

1849–1850

Much of Zachary Taylor's adulthood was spent not pursuing American politics. He served in uniform for nearly 40 years, and led the U.S. Army through a war with Mexico during the 1840s.

During Taylor's short presidency of 16 months (he died while in office), the U.S. was split over the controversy of extending slavery into the western territories. Despite the fact that Taylor was a large slaveholder himself, he did not stand in the way of admitting California as a free state and New Mexico as a free territory.

Born on November 24, 1784, Taylor was the seventh president born in Virginia, near Barboursville. He was one of nine children born to Richard and Sarah Taylor, a prominent Virginia plantation family. His father served in the Revolutionary War as an officer. When Richard received land in Kentucky from the federal government as a payment for his Revolutionary War service, he and his family moved across the Appalachian Mountains in 1785 and settled in the Ohio Country. There young Zachary grew up on the frontier. His schooling was limited to a handful of tutors.

Raised on stories of the American Revolution and of struggles with Indians, Taylor joined the army in his early 20s and soon became an officer. In 1810, he met and married Margaret Mackall Smith with whom he had six children. (One daughter, Sarah, would later marry Jefferson Davis, who would one day be the president of the Confederacy.)

Taylor's military career later included fighting during the War of 1812, the Black Hawk War, and the Mexican War. He achieved the rank of brigadier general in 1838. His generalship during the Mexican War (1846–47) brought him national attention.

His victories against the Mexican army included battles at Palo Alto, Matamoros, and Monterrey. His greatest win, however, was over the Mexican general, Santa Anna, at the Battle of Buena Vista where his army was outnumbered at least four to one.

In 1848, the Whig Party nominated him as their presidential candidate, and he won the race against Democrat Lewis Cass and Free Soil candidate, Martin Van Buren.

Lacking political experience, President Taylor relied on advice from a number of associates and friends. The chief issue—the expansion of slavery—dominated his 16-month tenure in the White House. Taylor encouraged the admission of California as a free state. While southerners opposed this, Taylor would not waver. Refusing to compromise on the issue, Taylor did not live to see California admitted. He became ill and died on July 9, 1850.

Review and Write

Taylor represented yet another general who was chosen to run as a Whig candidate for president. Why do you think the Whigs turned so often to military leaders as their candidates?

Millard Fillmore

1850–1853

In the summer of 1850, for only the second time in United States history, a vice president rose to the presidency upon the death of the chief executive.

Zachary Taylor's vice president, Millard Fillmore, completed Taylor's term. Like Taylor's, Fillmore's presidency was troubled by the controversy over the extension of slavery into the western territories.

Throughout his political career, Fillmore was opposed to slavery. While serving as vice president, he presided over the Senate debates over admitting California into the Union as a free state. But the compromise negotiated in the Senate to restrict slavery from California included a strong fugitive slave law, which allowed southerners to recover slaves who had escaped to the North.

Fillmore's strong desire to hold the Union together led him to support the Compromise of 1850, including its fugitive slave law. Although his was a position unpopular among northerners (and probably cost him the Whig nomination for president in 1852), he stood by his convictions and managed to postpone the Civil War by an entire decade.

As a youth, Fillmore seemed an unlikely candidate for the U.S. presidency. He was born in the frontier town of Locke, New York, on January 7, 1800. His early education was limited and he was apprenticed to a firm of cloth makers at age 14. After purchasing his freedom from the apprenticeship, he decided to receive more schooling. One of his tutors, Abigail

Powers, later became his wife. They had two children. In time, Fillmore became a lawyer.

In 1828, Fillmore was elected to the New York House of Representatives and four years later to the U.S. House of Representatives. He served four terms in the House. During the 1848 campaign for president, Fillmore was chosen as the running mate for presidential candidate, Zachary Taylor. The pair won the election.

Following Taylor's death in the summer of 1850, President Fillmore publicly supported a national compromise on slavery. He and his cabinet—he replaced Taylor men who had opposed compromising—drafted the Compromise of 1850. California was admitted to the Union under the compromise, the slave trade in the nation's capital ended, and New Mexico and Utah were organized without mentioning slavery.

After the Whigs dumped him for another term in 1852, Fillmore returned to law practice. He ran as a Whig candidate for the presidency in 1856 and lost. Fillmore died of a stroke on March 8, 1874.

Review and Write

Do you think Fillmore was right in supporting the Compromise of 1850 even though he was personally opposed to slavery? Explain your answer.

Franklin Pierce

1853–1857

The Rise of Franklin Pierce

When 48-year-old, New Hampshire-born Franklin Pierce was elected president in 1852, he was the youngest man to hold the office to that date. He was an impressive man, an excellent speaker who was well-respected in his home state as a politician and military veteran. Yet when he ran for the presidency, he was a virtual unknown across the country. His single term as chief executive was a difficult one for the United States. The issue of slavery and its territorial expansion was ripping the country apart. Despite the country's general prosperity, Pierce was forced to focus on a divided citizenry.

He was born in Hillsboro, New Hampshire, on November 23, 1804. His father, Benjamin Pierce, had fought in the Revolutionary War and served as governor of New Hampshire. Franklin's younger years were happily spent with his eight brothers and sisters. As a young teen, he attended Bowdoin College. One of his classmates was Nathaniel Hawthorne, who later became an important American author.

Although his early college grades were poor, Pierce eventually worked hard, applied himself to his studies, and graduated third in his class. Over the next few years he studied law and was admitted to the bar in 1827.

He entered politics in 1829 as a Jacksonian Democrat, being elected to the New Hampshire House. After two terms, he was elected to the U.S. House of Representatives. Within four years, he was elected to the Senate as its youngest member.

While Pierce's career in the House and the Senate were politically satisfying, they were difficult years for him and his wife. Mrs. Pierce did not like Washington life. She was ill with tuberculosis and prone to depression. (Two of her children had died young, which saddened her deeply.) Jane was a shy person and did not like to mingle at political gatherings. She finally convinced Franklin to abandon his political career in 1842 and return to New Hampshire.

But Washington politics soon came calling. In 1846, Pierce was chosen by President Polk as his attorney general. He refused the offer, as well as a Senate seat. Pierce was more interested in serving in the military during the approaching Mexican War. He was commissioned by Polk as a colonel in the U.S. Army and was later promoted to brigadier general. He distinguished himself in battle, despite a leg injury.

After the war, Pierce took up his law practice in Concord, New Hampshire. His continuing involvement in Democratic politics placed him at the center of the Democratic convention in 1852. The party was split regionally and none of the more well known men—including Stephen Douglas of Illinois and Lewis Cass—were able to win the party's nomination. Eventually, Pierce was nominated as a compromise candidate.

The Presidency of Franklin Pierce

In 1852, Pierce defeated the Whig candidate, General Winfield Scott. (Ironically, Pierce had served directly under General Scott's command during the Mexican War.)

Since he had been chosen as a compromise candidate for his party, Pierce was sensitive to the divisions splitting the country over slavery. His cabinet included three southerners and three northerners. Among them was southerner, Jefferson Davis, who served as his secretary of war. Davis would later become the president of the Confederacy during the Civil War. The mix of these cabinet members made for a volatility in Pierce's administration.

Personal problems again plagued Pierce's national politics. Just two months before his inauguration, Franklin Pierce and his fragile wife witnessed the death of their 11-year-old son in a railroad accident. Mrs. Pierce had opposed her husband's presidential aspirations and fell into a deep depression during their first two years in the White House.

Slavery dominated the Pierce administration. The issue of slavery in the new territory of Kansas led to extreme violence and killing. Pierce had supported the Kansas-Nebraska bill which had opened up the territory to possible slavery. Pierce found himself unable to adequately deal with the violence taking place in Kansas.

During his presidency, Pierce was an expansionist in foreign policy. His administration negotiated the purchase of land comprising the southwestern portion of modern-day Arizona for the Union. (His purpose was to provide a southern route for a proposed transcontinental railroad to California.) Despite successes such as the Gadsden Purchase in 1853, and a successful trade treaty with Japan, Pierce's presidency was forestalled by the debate over slavery.

In 1856, the Democratic Party was badly split over slavery. Pierce had failed to keep the party together and was not considered a viable candidate for a second presidential term. The party selected another northerner—this time from Pennsylvania—James Buchanan.

Pierce and his wife traveled abroad to Europe for two years after his presidency, but Jane's health never fully returned. They retired to their home in Massachusetts, where Jane died in 1863.

Former President Pierce lived to see the Civil War begin and end. Despite his northern roots, he did not support President Lincoln's leadership during the war. Pierce felt Lincoln should have avoided war with the seceded southern states. Pierce died in 1869.

Review and Write

1. The overarching issue during the Pierce administration was the issue of slavery and its expansion. How did Pierce attempt to deal with this issue? Was he successful? Explain.

_____

_____

_____

_____

_____

2. Pierce faced several personal crises during his political career involving his wife and family. Give some examples.

_____

_____

_____

_____

_____

_____

James Buchanan

1857–1861

The Rise of James Buchanan

Few presidents before James Buchanan came to the White House with more practical political experience than he did. By the time he was elected to the highest office in the land in 1856 at the age of 65, he had spent 40 years as a congressman, senator, foreign diplomat to both Russia and Great Britain, and secretary of state.

Yet the years of the Buchanan presidency were difficult for him and the nation. The course of conflict was well established between the north and south over the issues of slavery and its expansion into western territories. In addition, the United States suffered through a severe depression beginning in 1857. Despite Buchanan's previous extensive political and diplomatic experience, it did not help him cope with the problems which darkened his tenure in office.

His father migrated to America from Ireland just a few years before James Buchanan's birth on April 23, 1791. Born near Mercersburg, Pennsylvania, in a log cabin, Buchanan was raised with a strong sense of religion, patriotism, and love of learning. He attended Dickinson College and graduated in 1809 with honors. (Earlier in his college years, he had been expelled for violating the college rules.) He took up the practice of law in 1813. Over the years, he became a wealthy attorney.

He served during the War of 1812 as a private and helped defend the city of Baltimore in 1814. Back home, he was elected to the Pennsylvania assembly as a Federalist. In 1816, he left politics and returned to his legal practice in Lancaster, Pennsylvania. A few years later, he began courting a young girl named Ann Coleman. Family criticism of Buchanan caused her to break off the engagement. A week later, she died; rumors claimed she committed suicide, although it was never proven. Buchanan grieved her death all of his life. He never married. In part to ease his personal pain, Buchanan returned to politics and was elected to the U.S. House of Representatives in 1820. He began his early public and political career as a Federalist, but his party did not survive long past the War of 1812.

With the collapse of the Federalist Party, Buchanan turned to the Democratic Party and became a supporter of Andrew Jackson. Despite Jackson's loss of the 1824 election against John Quincy Adams, Buchanan remained a stalwart Jackson man.

When Jackson was elected to the presidency in 1828, he rewarded Buchanan's support by appointing him minister to Russia. Within a few years, Buchanan successfully negotiated the first commercial treaty between the U.S. and Russia. He did not enjoy living in Russia, however, and returned to the United States after only two years abroad.

Additional political success followed for Buchanan. From 1834 to 1845, he served as a U.S. Senator from Pennsylvania. When Polk was elected president, he appointed Buchanan as secretary of state.

Years of Crisis

During the Polk administration, Buchanan negotiated with Mexico over the southwest land cession following the Mexican War. Under this agreement, the U.S. annexed from Mexico all of the southwest region from California to Texas.

Diplomatically, Buchanan also became involved in negotiating a clearer border between the United States and Canada. He believed that the United States should have control of the Oregon Country and sought diplomacy to help bring Oregon under American domination.

By the early 1850s, Buchanan began to campaign for the presidency. He failed to gain the nomination in 1852. When his rival for the Democratic nomination, Franklin Pierce, won the election of 1852, he appointed Buchanan to yet another diplomatic position, this time as minister to Great Britain.

In 1856, Buchanan was again prepared to run for the Democratic nomination for president. He was chosen by his party because he had been out of the country prior to 1856, and had not taken a public position on the Kansas-Nebraska Act— a highly controversial piece of legislation concerning the potential expansion of slavery into both the Kansas and Nebraska Territories. (The Democratic Party was split north and south over this issue.) Buchanan won the election over his Republican challenger, John C. Fremont, of California.

During his administration, Buchanan attempted to avoid direct conflict over the issue of the expansion of slavery. He worked hard to unite the Democratic Party over this issue, but failed. He endorsed the concept of popular sovereignty which allowed for the existence of slavery in any western territory where a majority of voters agreed they wanted it. His support of a pro-slavery state government for Kansas alienated many northerners. As the nation drifted toward war, Buchanan was unable to change the minds of his countrymen.

Buchanan proposed a positive agenda for America during his presidency—one designed to encourage economic and regional growth. He supported the build-up of the U.S. military, the construction of a transcontinental railroad, and the construction of a canal across Central America. But Congress did not cooperate with him on these issues.

Frustrated, Buchanan did not seek his own renomination for the presidency in 1860. After the election of Abraham Lincoln to the presidency in the fall of 1860, Buchanan watched helplessly as southern states began to secede from the Union. He did nothing to stop these newly separated Confederate states. He did not believe that states had the right to secede, but also recognized that there was little he could do under the Constitution to keep it from happening.

When the Civil War broke out, he threw his support to Lincoln. Buchanan lived to see the Union restored and died in 1868 at the age of 77.

Review and Write

1. What political experience did Buchanan have prior to his election to the presidency in 1856?

_____

_____

_____

_____

2. What major problems did Buchanan face as president of the United States?

_____

_____

_____

_____

Abraham Lincoln

1861–1865

Frontier Youth

Perhaps no man faced more or greater challenges as president than did Abraham Lincoln. Today, he is regarded as one of the greatest presidents of the United States, but this honor was won at great personal cost.

The controversies which had raged across the U.S. for half a century finally came to a head in the early 1860s, leading the nation into Civil War, just as Abraham Lincoln was preparing to take office as the chief executive. Four years of bloody, divisive war marred his presidency from its beginning. Yet in the end, Lincoln restored the fractured Union, and prepared to witness the return of the Confederate states back into a new and morally stronger nation.

He penned the Emancipation Proclamation in 1863, which led to the dissolution of slavery in America. Through his courageous, and sometimes controversial, decisions, the United States not only weathered the challenge of the Civil War, but emerged, in the words of Lincoln's famous Gettysburg Address, with a "new birth of freedom." Truly, Lincoln stands tall as one of the greatest of America's leaders.

Abraham Lincoln was born in a log cabin in Larue County, Kentucky, on February 12, 1809. His family moved from the log cabin two years later, but just ten miles away. In 1816, Lincoln's father, Thomas, decided to move his family to Indiana.

Life was hard there, for Indiana was still frontier country. The Lincolns spent their first winter in a three-sided lean-to cabin made of split logs called a half-faced camp. They were constantly exposed to the winter weather and maintained a campfire on the open side of their cabin at all times. This kept wild animals away and provided warmth.

Although he was young, Lincoln was expected to work hard, complete chores, and help on the farm. By age eight, he was big enough to wield an ax. The family was struck with tragedy when Abraham's mother, Nancy, died in 1818, of what is believed to have been milk sickness. The Lincolns continued on without her until the next year when Abraham's father remarried a women from Kentucky, Sarah Bush Johnston. She brought with her three children from an earlier marriage and helped fill the Lincoln home with happiness. Through these wilderness years, young Lincoln grew into manhood. Later in life, he claimed of his stepmother, "All that I am or ever hope to be I owe to her."

During these formative years, Lincoln received little formal schooling. At age 22, He left home, hired by a trader to help take a flatboat down the Ohio and Mississippi rivers to New Orleans. The trader later hired Lincoln to work in his general store in the village of New Salem in Illinois. Illinois remained Lincoln's home for the next 30 years.

The Rise of Abraham Lincoln

The next several years were formative for young Lincoln. His work as a store clerk brought little income, but he spent much of his time borrowing books and reading the classics. In 1832, he participated in the Black Hawk War, but saw no action. The following year, Lincoln was appointed postmaster of New Salem; later, he worked as a surveyor.

In 1834, he ran in his first political race for the state legislature and won, serving four terms as a Whig. Through these years, Lincoln studied law and received his license to practice in 1836. For the next several years, Lincoln shared a practice with several different partners.

In 1846, Lincoln ran for the U.S. House of Representatives as a Whig and again won. After two years, he left the House and returned to the law. By the late 1840s and early 50s, Lincoln was a well-known lawyer in Illinois and was becoming prosperous. He had married a woman ten years younger than he, Mary Todd, in 1842. The Lincolns had four boys.

By 1854, Lincoln was drawn back into politics once more. His concern over the proposed Kansas-Nebraska bill—introduced in Congress by Illinois senator, Stephen Douglas, to allow slavery in a non-slave territory—drove Lincoln to campaign on behalf of candidates opposed to the bill.

In 1858, Lincoln was prepared to run against Stephen Douglas himself for his senate seat. By this time, Lincoln was a member of a new political party—the Republicans. Speaking after his nomination, Lincoln said concerning the future of slavery in America, "A house divided against itself cannot stand. I believe this government cannot endure, permanently half slave and half free . . . It will become all one thing, or all the other." (Lincoln hated slavery and deplored its movement into free territories.)

The campaign produced the famous Lincoln-Douglas debates, which focused on the extension of slavery into the territories, but Lincoln lost the election. However, he was becoming a known Republican figure across the north. Two years later, during the Republican national convention in Chicago, Lincoln was nominated as the presidential candidate for the party. Out of four candidates (including Democrat Stephen Douglas), Lincoln was elected. Ahead of him stretched four long years of Civil War.

The Presidency of Abraham Lincoln

In the days following Lincoln's election in November 1860, the country began to fall apart at the seams. States continued to secede from the United States beginning with South Carolina in December. When Lincoln took office in March 1861, six additional states had seceded. In all, 11 states left the Union by early summer. Difficult days lay ahead for President Lincoln.

The Inauguration of President Lincoln

In his inauguration speech on March 4, 1861, Lincoln spoke to the southern states in secession. He assured them that as president he had no plans to interfere with southern slavery where it existed (a right he recognized under the Constitution). He appealed to the southern states to return to the Union and reminded southerners that they, as citizens of the United States, shared a history with the North. Lincoln said in his speech that Americans are all bound by the "mystic chords of memory, stretching from every battlefield and patriot grave to every living heart . . . over this broad land."

While appealing for the South's return, Lincoln also announced to the southern states that he did not wish for war and that his desire was to hold the Union together. He was soon concerned about the federal forts in southern states. He announced he would supply food and provisions to one in need—Fort Sumter in Charleston Harbor, South Carolina.

Rather than allow the fort to be resupplied, Confederate forces bombarded the island installation on April 12, 1861—the first shots fired of the Civil War.

With the war on, Lincoln called up state militia troops to defend the Union. He also called for 75,000 men to enlist for military duty. Lincoln ordered a blockade of all southern ports, but his navy did not include enough ships for the blockade to be immediately effective.

Some of Lincoln's early decisions were controversial. He authorized military spending before Congress approved. He arrested alleged Confederate sympathizers and held them without trial. One of Lincoln's immediate concerns was a war strategy. He received much pressure to order the U.S. army to march south from Washington, D.C., to the new Confederate capital of Richmond, Virginia, just 100 miles away. Lincoln gave in to this expectation, and Union and Confederate troops faced one another in the first battle of Bull Run on July 21, 1861.

When the Union forces lost the battle, it became clear that this war was not going to be easily won. Lincoln spent three years searching for a general who could defeat the southern states. Generals such as George B. McClellan, chosen by Lincoln in the summer of 1861, proved efficient in organizing the army, but ineffective in battle.

Lincoln and the Civil War

While the Battle of Antietam, fought on September 17, 1862 (the bloodiest day of the war), was a clear McClellan win, it would be his last. McClellan's cautiousness in battle angered Lincoln. After McClellan failed to aggressively pursue the retreating Confederate troops, Lincoln replaced him with General Ambrose Burnside. Other battles were disasters for the North: Second Bull Run (August 1862); the Seven Days campaign (June—July 1862); Fredericksburg (December 1862); and Chancellorsville (May 1863)—the latter serving as Robert E. Lee's greatest victory of the war.

Following the Antietam victory, President Lincoln issued the Emancipation Proclamation. He declared that the slaves in all rebellious or seceded states were to be freed as of January 1, 1863. This noble document did not attempt to end slavery but it did change the motivations for the war. Northerners were, at least in part, fighting a war against the South, which would ultimately free black slaves. Now Lincoln was intending to fight a war for two reasons—restoring the Union, and emancipating slaves. This decision was met with some hostility across the North, but it served as the beginning of the process of eliminating slavery from American soil. By 1865, the U.S. Congress ratified the 13th Amendment to the U.S. Constitution, ending slavery in America.

Lincoln was much criticized during the war. Newspapers jeered and condemned his leadership, especially following disastrous losses on the battlefield. Yet he doggedly remained true to his goal of bringing the Union together again. Finally a victory in July 1863, at Gettysburg, brought a turning point to the war.

The Battle at Gettysburg

On April 9, 1865, Lee surrendered to Grant at Appomattox Court House in Virginia.

Personally, Lincoln and his family suffered much tragedy during the war. The war preoccupied him day and night, putting enormous strains on his family life. His wife, Mary, was under constant suspicion from Lincoln's critics, since she was a southerner from Kentucky whose family owned slaves. She had several brothers who served in the Confederacy. In February 1862, Lincoln's son William died. The Lincolns were deeply grieved by the loss, and the president was so sorrowful that he had his son's grave dug up on two occasions so he could once more look at Willie's face.

Following Antietam, additional northern victories—especially those won by a tireless northern campaigner named Ulysses S. Grant—brought new direction to the war. On occasion, Lincoln followed up military victories with political victories. After the Battle of Antietam, he announced his Emancipation Proclamation, which began freeing slaves in secession states.

After the successful northern victory at Gettysburg, Lincoln attended the dedication of a national cemetery in that small, Pennsylvania town. There he delivered his Gettysburg Address, explaining that this nation shall have a new birth of freedom. With this speech, Americans began to think of their country as a nation rather than as a union. No longer would any state seriously consider secession from the United States.

By 1864, the war was turning in favor of the North. Through the efforts of General Ulysses Grant, General Lee and the Confederacy were ultimately defeated in the spring of 1865. But the joy of victory for the North was mitigated by the tragic assassination of Lincoln by a Washington actor named John Wilkes Booth. Sadly, the president who had guided his people through the worst conflict America has ever seen was himself one of the war's final casualties.

Review and Write

1. Describe young Abraham's pioneer experiences growing up on the frontier.

2. What successes and failures did Lincoln face in his professional life before being elected president of the United States?

Andrew Johnson

1865–1869

The Rise of Andrew Johnson

To some Americans, the spring of 1865 was the worst of times. The American Civil War had just ended with its death toll of over 600,000 American soldiers on both sides. A zealous southern supporter, the actor John W. Booth, had killed President Lincoln days after the surrender of Robert E. Lee to General Grant.

The country was divided, and the years ahead were filled with animosity, political struggle, and repairing the wounds of war. With Lincoln's death, Vice President Andrew Johnson prepared to lead the nation. But his presidency became one of the most unpopular in American history. Johnson served only one term as president against the backdrop of the post-Civil War years—the period of Reconstruction (1865–1877) during which the Republican-controlled Congress attempted to determine the direction of the nation. Clashes between the chief executive and the radical Republicans in Congress eventually lead to a showdown and Johnson faced impeachment charges—the first American president ever to do so.

As with Abraham Lincoln, Andrew Johnson came from humble origins. He was born on December 29, 1808, in Raleigh, North Carolina. His father, Jacob, was a handyman in a local tavern and his mother, Mary McDonough, a tavern maid. Andrew barely knew his father, for he died while trying to save a drowning man when his son was only three years old. His mother supplemented the family's income by working as a seamstress and weaver. Perhaps this led young Andrew to become apprenticed to a tailor at age 14.

Andrew never attended school but learned to read from the foreman of his apprentice shop. He did not finish his six-year apprenticeship; instead, he left after two years. Soon he set himself up in his own tailor shop in Laurens Court House, South Carolina.

In 1825, he moved to Tennessee, and a year later moved his family (his mother, stepfather, and older brother) to Tennessee as well. The following year, he married Eliza McCardle, a shoemaker's daughter. Eliza probably helped teach Johnson how to write. The Johnsons produced five children.

Within the next three years, Johnson became involved in Tennessee politics. In 1828, the same year Jackson was elected president, Johnson won a local race for town alderman. Within ten years, he had served as Greeneville's mayor and as a member of the Tennessee House. In 1841, he was elected to the state senate; two years later, he was elected to the U.S. House of Representatives where he served until 1851. But his most significant political service lay ahead.

The Presidency of Andrew Johnson

After serving a term as Tennessee governor, Johnson was elected to the U.S. Senate. As a senator, he supported the passage of the Homestead Act, which granted free land to western settlers. In 1860, when southern states began seceding from the Union, Johnson, a southerner, did not support their efforts, denouncing all Confederates as traitors to the Union. In fact, Johnson was the only southern senator not resign from Congress.

When Union forces took political control of Tennessee in 1862, Lincoln appointed Johnson as the military governor. Johnson proved so loyal to the Union that he was named Lincoln's vice-presidential running mate for the 1864 election. Only six weeks after Lincoln's second inauguration, he was assassinated, and Johnson found himself a southern president amid a hostile camp of northern congressmen.

Johnson's immediate goal as president was to implement the Reconstruction policies of Abraham Lincoln. Lincoln had not intended to punish Confederate leaders, nor did Johnson.

During the spring of 1865, President Johnson began to use his executive power to help restore and heal the bitterly divided nation. He was lenient toward the South. He granted amnesty and a pardon to Confederate soldiers or supporters who agreed to pledge loyalty to the United States. Johnson also promised to recognize their property rights with the exception of restoring their slaves.

Johnson's plan had many exceptions and people could appeal to the president for a direct pardon from him. By the fall of 1865, Johnson was granting presidential pardons to approximately 100 people daily. He rarely denied a pardon to anyone.

Soon Johnson and the radical Republicans in Congress were at odds. Johnson was not open to granting southern blacks power (he appears to have been quite racist). This caused concern on behalf of Republicans in Congress. When they attempted to pass a Civil Rights bill in 1866, he vetoed it.

When Johnson faced his Republican challengers, they attempted to remove him from office. In 1867, Republican congressmen passed the Tenure of Office Act, which was designed to restrict Johnson's presidential power. He challenged their authority and the Republicans rallied together to face his challenge.

On February 24, 1868, the House voted to impeach Johnson by a vote of 126 to 47. The charges against Johnson included eleven counts of high crimes and misdemeanors. But the Senate failed to remove him from office by one vote. (Privately, Johnson made it clear to Congress that he would uphold and support the Reconstruction Acts passed by Congress.) His political career ruined, Johnson did not run for the presidency in 1868.

Despite some foreign policy successes by the Johnson administration, including the purchase of Alaska from the Russians in 1867 for $7.2 million, the Johnson presidency is often considered a failure. However, one of his final acts as president was to pardon all southerners who had fought in the Civil War. In the end, he had his way. Johnson died in 1875 of a stroke.

Review and Write

1. Andrew Johnson came from humble beginnings, yet managed to become president of the United States. Is it possible for someone of such beginnings to become president today? Why or why not?

_____

_____

_____

2. The clash between presidential power and Congressional power came to a head in 1867 when the Republican-controlled Congress attempted to remove Johnson from the presidency. Do you think that effort was a reasonable response to Johnson's politics? Why or why not?

_____

_____

Ulysses S. Grant

1869–1877

The Making of Ulysses S. Grant

As had other presidents before him, Ulysses S. Grant formed his national reputation first as a general on the battlefield, then as a political figure. As the general who brought the Union to victory, Grant was a hero. The American people chose to show their respect and admiration for the great general by electing him president to two terms beginning in 1868.

But Grant proved to be much less capable as a president than he had been as a soldier. Although considered personally honest, Grant's administration was one of the most corrupt in U.S. history.

He was the first child of Jesse and Hannah Simpson Grant, born April 27, 1822, in Point Peasant, Ohio, on the Ohio River. He was named Hiram Ulysses Grant. His father was a leather tanner, but young Ulysses did not take to the family business. He was sickened by the sight of blood, whether animal or human. Ulysses was skilled with horses, however, and became known for his kindness to them.

He attended several schools and academies growing up. Then, at age 17, he was selected by an Ohio congressman to a position at the military academy at West Point. It was that congressman who accidentally changed Grant's name to Ulysses S. Grant, the name he wrote on the West Point application. At the academy, the name stuck. He kept it the rest of his life.

Grant was a reluctant student at West Point, never intending to make the military his life. He did manage to graduate in 1843 and was commissioned as a second lieutenant. Over the next three years, Grant was stationed in St. Louis, Louisiana, and Texas. While in St. Louis, Grant met Julia Dent. They married in 1848.

Grant distinguished himself in 1847 during the American war with Mexico. He served in an artillery unit and participated in the assault on Mexico City. Grant's experiences in the Mexico conflict served him well during the Civil War.

For the first six years of their marriage, Grant continued his military career and was often separated from Julia. He performed his military duties at garrisons in Detroit and Sackets Harbor, N.Y. In 1852, he was assigned to duty at Fort Vancouver in the Oregon Country. Separated from his wife and family, Grant was often sad and lonely. At times, he drank too heavily. The next year he was promoted to the rank of captain and was stationed at Fort Humboldt in California. Still separated from his family, he was no happier there. In 1854, he resigned his army commission.

For the next six years, the Grants struggled along as Ulysses went from job to job. He enjoyed but failed at farming, working land near St. Louis, Missouri, which was given to him by his father-in-law.

Grant worked in a real estate office, served in the U.S. Customs House, and as a clerk in his own father's store. These were years of poverty for the Grants. When the Civil War came in 1861, Grant returned to military service.

The Presidency of Ulysses S. Grant

During the war, Grant distinguished himself as a skilled and capable military commander. He met the enemy with determination and calm, and was capable of making decisions under pressure. His victories in Illinois, Tennessee, and Mississippi gained him a national reputation. His siege and recapture of the southern city of Vicksburg won him the attention of the war department and of President Lincoln.

By early 1864, Grant was promoted by Lincoln to lieutenant general and placed in command of all Union forces. From May 4 to June 18, Grant fought directly against the greatest of Confederate generals, Robert E. Lee. These weeks of fighting produced bitter battles as the two men and their armies slugged their way across Virginia. From the Chancellorsville Wilderness to Spotsylvania to Cold Harbor to Petersburg, Grant relentlessly fought a grinding war of attrition with Lee, stacking up casualties numbering in the tens of thousands.

But Grant's dogged determination won out in the end. By the summer of 1864, Grant had halted the campaigns of Confederate General Robert E. Lee. The following spring, Lee surrendered to Grant. The Civil War was over and Grant was the hero.

In 1868, the Republican Party chose Grant as their presidential candidate. He defeated New York governor, Horatio Seymour. The Grant presidency was soon beset with corruption at the hands of many in his administration. Unscrupulous political appointees took bribes and made secret deals and contracts.

Grant worked hard to restore the nation divided by the Civil War. He convinced congressmen to pardon Confederate leaders. The president also worked on behalf of Negro rights in the South. When the Ku Klux Klan threatened Negroes, Grant attempted to use federal troops to protect the former slaves.

While Grant's second term was marred by a significant economic depression that began in 1873, he also presided over the completion of the transcontinental railroad, the invention of the telephone, and the establishment of the first national park—Yellowstone.

In retirement, Grant invested his savings of approximately $100,000 with a dishonest banker. The firm was known as Grant & Ward, and his son, Ulysses, Jr. was part of the company. But Grant's partner, Ferdinand Ward, proved to be dishonest and the bank failed. By 1884, Grant was penniless.

He spent his final days penning his memoirs. He sold the rights to his life's story to the great American writer, Mark Twain, who agreed to publish the work. By 1885, Grant was dying of throat cancer and struggling with his illness as he hastily wrote his memoirs. He moved with his family to the Adirondack Mountains, where the mountain air helped him with his breathing. There he died on July 23, 1885.

His autobiography was a great financial success, which provided his family with an income of $500,000.

Review and Write

1. Grant was a failure in life perhaps more often than he was a success. List some examples of his personal failures.

_____

_____

_____

_____

2. How did Grant's service during the Civil War lead to his presidency in 1868?

_____

_____

_____

Test II

Part I.

Multiple Choice.

Match the information at the left to the answers on the right. Place the letter of the correct answer in the spaces below.

1. Served as president during the Panic of 1837.
2. Was sometimes called Young Hickory to honor Andrew Jackson.
3. During his presidency, Congress passed the Compromise of 1850.
4. He and his wife witnessed the death of their son in a railroad accident.
5. Spoke out in the Senate in favor of abolishing the slave trade.
6. Fought successful military campaign during the War of 1812.
7. Encouraged a war with Mexico to acquire California.
8. Was unable or unwilling to halt the violence in Kansas.
9. First vice president to become chief executive after a president's death.
10. He and First Lady banned alcohol, dancing, and card-playing at the White House.
11. Fought in the War of 1812, the Black Hawk War, and the Mexican War.
12. Ran for president with the slogan "Tippecanoe and Tyler, too!"

A. James K. Polk
B. Zachary Taylor
C. Martin Van Buren
D. John Tyler
E. William Harrison
F. Franklin Pierce
G. Millard Fillmore

Answers:

1. ____ 2. ____ 3. ____ 4. ____ 5. ____ 6. ____ 7. ____ 8. ____ 9. ____ 10. ____ 11. ____ 12. ____

Part II.

Multiple Choice.

Match the information at the left to the answers on the right. Place the letter of the correct answer in the spaces below.

1. During his presidency, the United States experienced the 1857 depression.
2. Debated Stephen Douglas during the 1858 U.S. Senate race.
3. Worked as a tailor and was taught to write by his wife.
4. Graduated from West Point Military Academy.
5. His support of a pro-slavery government in Kansas alienated northerners.
6. During his presidency, the transcontinental railroad was completed.
7. Struggled in his search for a successful Union general during the Civil War.
8. America's first president to be impeached by the House.
9. Was born in Kentucky and his mother died of milk sickness.
10. Was assassinated by an actor named John Wilkes Booth.
11. Alaska was purchased from Russia during his administration.
12. Delivered an 1858 speech that said, "A house divided against itself cannot stand."

A. Abraham Lincoln
B. Ulysses S. Grant
C. James Buchanan
D. Andrew Johnson

Answers:

1. ____ 2. ____ 3. ____ 4. ____ 5. ____ 6. ____ 7. ____ 8. ____ 9. ____ 10. ____ 11. ____ 12. ____

Rutherford B. Hayes

1877–1881

The Rise of Rutherford B. Hayes

Rutherford Hayes is often remembered for two aspects of his presidency. The first, that he was elected through a questionable electoral process, and the second, that he ended the long-running Reconstruction period that had gripped the South since the end of the Civil War.

Yet Hayes and his administration are noteworthy for other reasons. His single term in office followed one of the most scandal-ridden administrations in American history. Hayes supported legislation which limited corruption in office and helped eliminate the spoils system which was common to American politics. This system often led to politicians replacing government bureaucrats with friends and political supporters, regardless of their qualifications.

Although he entered the White House under the cloud of a tricky election process, he created a presidency that brought him honor and respect. His basic political creed was, "He serves his party best who serves his country best."

Rutherford Birchard Hayes was born in Delaware, Ohio, on October 4, 1822. He was the fifth child of Rutherford Hayes, Jr. and Sophia Birchard Hayes, but his father died two months before Rutherford's birth. Only Rutherford and his sister, Fanny, survived childhood.

He attended schools in Ohio and Connecticut and enrolled in Kenyon College in Ohio in 1838. After graduating first in his class, Rutherford attended Harvard Law School, where he graduated and was admitted to the bar in 1845.

His early law career did not bring many clients and Hayes struggled financially. In 1852, he gained attention as a defense attorney in a widely publicized Ohio murder case after he saved his clients from being executed. During these years, Hayes was actively involved in the "Underground Railroad," helping slaves escape.

In December 1852, Hayes married Lucy Ware Webb, a college graduate and daughter of an Ohio doctor. She was a reformer who campaigned against slavery and favored the prohibition of alcohol. (She is best remembered for her ban on alcohol in the White House, a move which earned her the name "Lemonade Lucy.")

In 1858, Hayes served as chief attorney for the city of Cincinnati. When the Civil War began in 1861, Hayes enlisted and saw action during the war. Five times he was wounded in battle. During the war, Hayes was elected to the House of Representatives, but refused to take his seat until the war was over.

In 1867, he was elected to the governorship of Ohio, and was re-elected twice. Through that office, he campaigned for voting rights for blacks. His efforts to institute civil service reform in Ohio led to his nomination for president in 1876.

The 1876 election is remembered as one of the more controversial in American history. Hayes was nominated as the standard bearer of the Republican Party despite much division within the party. The party in 1876 was divided between those known as the *Half-Breeds* and the *Stalwarts*. The Stalwarts wanted to renominate President Grant for a third term, but Grant was unwilling to run. The two wings could not agree on a candidate. Hayes was chosen only as a last resort and was considered a compromise by both sides.

Hayes was nominated on the convention's seventh ballot and his running mate was House of Representatives member, William A. Wheeler, of New York. But the greater controversy of the 1876 election was yet to come.

The Presidency of Rutherford B. Hayes

With Hayes as the compromise Republican candidate, the Democrats selected Samuel J. Tilden, noted New York governor and well-known lawyer. He already had a well-founded reputation as one of the attorneys who had helped close down the corrupt practices in New York City of William Marcy Tweed.

Many did not expect Hayes to win the election. The Democrats had been gaining in political power for the previous two years and the Grant administration was known as corrupt. However, when the election was held, neither Hayes nor his Democratic opponent, New Yorker Samuel Tilden, received enough electoral votes to constitute a victory.

Immediately, a controversy unfolded. Four states submitted two sets of ballots—one Democratic and one Republican—and were therefore in dispute. Despite the fact that Tilden had received over 200,000 more popular votes than Hayes, and 19 more electoral votes, a Republican-dominated electoral commission declared Hayes the winner by granting him all 20 of the disputed electoral votes. The decision of the commission would be questioned by Hayes's opponents throughout his presidency.

As president, Hayes withdrew the last federal troops still occupying the Reconstruction South. He also instituted civil service reform in the federal government. He made appointments to his cabinet and other offices based on merit and qualification. He even appointed a southern Democrat to his cabinet.

Many of Hayes's efforts toward reform did not meet with the approval of members of Congress. Nor did they meet with the approval of the more corrupt elements of the Republican Party.

A persistent issue during the Hayes presidency related to the amount of paper money and silver in circulation. Such monies were questionable, since they were commonly not backed by gold. Hayes pursued a conservative monetary policy throughout his presidency, and even vetoed "cheap money" bills.

Hayes chose to serve only one term as president. He spent his final years in Ohio as a social reformer of education and prisons. He died on January 17, 1893.

Review and Write

1. How did Hayes show his support for blacks in his private and public life?

_____

_____

_____

_____

2. Hayes entered the White House under a cloud of controversy. Do you think he was a good president? Why or why not?

_____

_____

_____

_____

_____

_____

James A. Garfield

1881

The presidency of James A. Garfield was cut short by an assassin's bullet. As the fourth president to die in office and the second to be killed, Garfield's impact on the presidency was limited. Yet the trend of President Rutherford B. Hayes continued beyond Garfield's death, in part because Garfield was killed by a man who had sought a political office from him.

When the American people realized that political patronage had led to the death of the president, they were ready for change. And that change was brought about by Garfield's successor, Vice President Chester A. Arthur.

Ironically, Arthur had been the recipient of corrupt patronage all his political life. Yet, as president, he turned his back on the patronage system and campaigned on behalf of reform and civil service. Thus, political patronage and the need for reform of the civil service destroyed one presidency and created another.

James Abram Garfield was born in a log cabin on November 19, 1831, in Orange, Ohio. His parents were Abram and Eliza Ballou Garfield.

He attended the local school during his early years. For a short while, he worked as a canal worker, driving a team of horses. After attending several colleges, Garfield graduated from Williams College in 1856. He became a professor of languages and literature, and later became the president of Williams.

Garfield continued his education, studying law, and serving as a Disciples of Christ preacher. In 1858, he married Lucretia Rudolph, a former student. The next year, he was elected to the Ohio state senate.

When the Civil War broke out in 1861, Garfield became a field commander, and ended the war as a major general. He participated in the Battle of Shiloh in 1862, and Chickamauga in 1863. Returning to civilian life, Garfield was elected to the U.S. House of Representatives. He voted against President Johnson during the impeachment crisis.

In 1880, Garfield was elected to the U.S. Senate and before year's end was chosen as the Republican candidate for president. He held the office for only four months before he was shot on July 2, 1881, by an assassin named Charles Guiteau.

Guiteau had previously sought a government position in the Garfield administration in return for his political support. Garfield never even knew who Guiteau was. He remained alive for 80 days, but died on September 19, 1881.

Review and Write

President Hayes had established the practice of civil service testing for government jobs. How did Garfield's assassination reveal the need for such testing?

Chester A. Arthur

1881–1885

Upon President Garfield's assassination in 1881, Vice President Chester Arthur became president. A longtime New York politician, Arthur came to the White House with a reputation of corruption.

Yet, as president, Arthur redeemed himself of his political past and became one of the most honest presidents in our history.

Born on October 5, 1829, in Fairfield, Vermont, his parents were William and Malvina Stone Arthur. He was one of nine children. He attended Union College and graduated at age 18. Chester studied law and began practicing in New York City in 1853. He was a defender of civil rights. Through his pursuit of an 1855 case, blacks in New York City gained the right to ride on the city's streetcars.

In 1859, he married Ellen Lewis Herndon and they had three children. (Mrs. Arthur died in 1880 before her husband became president.)

By the 1860s, Arthur was deeply involved in New York Republican politics. His political involvement won him a post as New York engineer-in-chief that included an officership in the New York State militia of brigadier general. When the Civil War broke out, New York's governor placed Arthur over the quartermaster's office responsible for supplying and providing uniforms for New York militiamen. Such appointments were generally gained as political favors. As he became more involved in New York politics, Arthur became an appointee of New York Republican machine politics, gaining a position as collector of the port of New York City in 1871. From that post, Arthur doled out political patronage to supporters of the Republican Party.

Following his election in 1876, President Rutherford Hayes began implementing civil service reform, including a ban on government employees serving as political party officials. One such official was Chester Arthur of New York. Hayes had Arthur removed from his position as port collector in 1879.

In 1880, he gained the nomination as Garfield's running mate in the presidential election. When Garfield was shot and killed, Arthur was abruptly thrust into the highest office in the land. Although Arthur had spent years as a machine politician handing out political favors, as president, he supported the Pendleton Civil Service Act, which changed how government officials were selected.

He failed to gain the nomination for re-election in 1884 and died two years later of Bright's disease.

Review and Write

Chester Arthur appeared to pursue some noble goals as president despite his corrupt political background. What were some of those goals? Was he successful?

Grover Cleveland

1885–1889 and 1893–1897

The Rise of Grover Cleveland

He was known to his family members as Uncle Jumbo. Grover Cleveland, a large-framed man with a strong sense of humor, served with distinction as the only president to serve two non-consecutive terms as president. President Benjamin Harrison served the term between Cleveland's two. Cleveland is also remembered as the only Democrat to serve as president in the 50-year period between James Buchanan [1857-61] and Woodrow Wilson [1913-21].

Cleveland served his country during a time of momentous change in America. The nation was moving ahead economically as large corporations began to dominate production. The United States was growing more urban as millions of immigrants poured into the country from Eastern Europe. Americans of all sorts continued their movement to the West, homesteading the prairies and the plains. These were years of clear economic, social, and cultural change.

Although he was not able to provide direction for all the changes America was experiencing, Grover Cleveland provided honest leadership— something Republicans had struggled with since Abraham Lincoln.

He was born Stephen Grover Cleveland on March 18, 1837, in Caldwell, New Jersey. (He preferred his middle name from the time he was just a boy.) His parents were Richard Cleveland, a Presbyterian minister, and Ann Neal Cleveland. (The family had a relative who was the founder of Cleveland, Ohio.)

Grover was the youngest of nine children, who grew up relatively poor. He attended school during his younger years and became a teacher for awhile. (His father died when Grover was only 16.) At 17, Grover Cleveland moved to Buffalo, New York, and began to study law. He supported himself by working as a law clerk for four dollars a week. In 1859, he was admitted to the bar. He supported his family with his earnings.

Cleveland's early political career included serving as a Democratic Party ward worker, assistant district attorney, and mayor of Buffalo. As mayor, Cleveland attempted to clean up the corrupt city government. His reputation as an honest politician won him the governorship of New York in 1882.

By 1884, he was known nationally, and the Democratic Party selected him as their candidate for the presidency. His campaign against Republican, James Blaine, a Maine senator, was a malicious one. Blaine supporters accused Cleveland of fathering a child while unmarried, a claim which proved true. Yet Cleveland won the election by a slight majority of 23,000 votes.

While president, Cleveland pursued a reform agenda. He instructed his officials to cut waste and corruption in their departments. He forced dishonest railroad companies to return to the government any excess land granted them during periods of railroad construction. Cleveland opposed handing out pensions to veterans of the Civil War who claimed disability, even for ailments related to their war service. Such decisions did not make Cleveland popular in certain circles across America.

The Presidency of Grover Cleveland

Since Cleveland was a bachelor when he was elected, he had no First Lady to arrange social events. His younger sister Rose served as social hostess. In 1886, Cleveland married a 21-year-old woman named Frances Folsom. He had known her for years. Her father had been one of Cleveland's law partners and, when her father died, Frances became Cleveland's ward. Cleveland's marriage while president made him the only president to marry in the White House.

Despite the differences in their ages (Cleveland was 49 to her 21), the marriage endured and produced five children. Following Cleveland's death in 1908, his wife lived 40 more years, dying in 1947. (She remarried in 1913.)

One of the heated issues of the period was the continuing debate over the money supply in America and the distribution of "cheap money" such as paper greenbacks and silver. Cleveland pursued a sound monetary policy, asking Congress to adopt a strict gold standard and to repeal acts which caused the federal government to regularly purchase silver at inflated prices.

Cleveland ran for re-election in 1888. His opponent was Benjamin Harrison, the Republican candidate. The chief issue of the campaign was tariff rates. While Cleveland was not an unpopular president in general, some of his policies were not liked by specific interest groups, such as veterans, farmers, and factory owners. Both he and Harrison pursued lackluster campaigns. Although Cleveland polled more popular votes than Harrison, his opponent won more electoral votes, taking the election.

After failing to win the election in 1888, Cleveland spent the next four years practicing law in New York City. As consumer prices increased during the Harrison years, and tariff rates continued to edge upward, Cleveland became highly critical of the Democratic administration.

He ran again in 1892 and won against incumbent Republican president, Benjamin Harrison. Although Cleveland began his second term amid great national popularity, he soon found himself presiding over a nation in deep financial depression, beginning in 1893. It lasted through his entire term. When the country faced a serious gold drain due to a pullout of European investors in the U.S. economy, he struck a deal with Wall Street financiers to provide gold for the nation's dwindling reserves. The move probably saved the nation's economy, which made a gradual recovery.

While financial issues dominated the Cleveland administration at home, the United States began to pursue foreign policy goals. Cleveland inherited a bill before Congress to annex the Hawaiian Islands. Cleveland did not support the annexation and did not pursue the passage of the treaty.

Cleveland became involved in a boundary dispute in South America between Venezuela and Great Britain. When Cleveland seemed to threaten American military involvement in the affair, Great Britain agreed to allow an arbitration board to decide the issue at hand. The crisis passed.

In 1896, Cleveland chose not to seek another term. In retirement, he lived in Princeton, New Jersey. There he wrote and published some of his lectures. He served as a trustee of Princeton. Cleveland died on June 24, 1908, after an illness of three months.

Review and Write

On his death bed, Cleveland's last words were, "I have tried so hard to do right." How did his politics—including those of his presidency— reveal the efforts of a man who is seeking to accomplish good things?

_____

_____

_____

Benjamin Harrison

1889–1893

The Rise of Benjamin Harrison

Benjamin Harrison was not the first member of his family to make a contribution to American history. In colonial America, early Harrisons had served as burgesses and militia colonels. His great-grandfather, another Benjamin Harrison, was a signer of the Declaration of Independence. His grandfather William Henry Harrison, was himself president in 1840. Benjamin's father had served in the U.S. Congress.

As president, Benjamin Harrison was prudent, strong, principled, and fair. His administration helped move the presidency and the nation into the world arena as a major economic and military power.

One of his passions as president was a keen respect for the American flag. Through his example, Americans gained a new reverence for this national symbol. He ordered the flag to be flown over the White House, as well as other federal buildings. With his encouragement, nearly every public school in America began to raise the flag daily.

Benjamin Harrison was born on August 20, 1833, in North Bend, Ohio. He was one of ten children born to John Scott Harrison and Elizabeth Irwin Harrison. He grew up on a farm.

While attending Farmers' College in Cincinnati, he met Caroline Lavinia Scott. They married in 1853 after Benjamin's graduation from Miami University

the previous year. They had two children. The Harrison's were religious people, and Benjamin served as a deacon and later an elder of the Presbyterian Church.

In 1854, Benjamin Harrison was admitted to the bar and began practicing law in Indianapolis. Against his father's advice, Harrison got involved in politics, and was elected city attorney of Indianapolis in 1857.

During the Civil War, Harrison raised a regiment of Indiana volunteers. He was known by his men as "Little Ben" due to his height (5 feet 6 inches tall). The 70th regiment fought in several battles and Harrison rose to the rank of brigadier general. Following the war, Harrison returned to practicing law and Indiana politics. He ran for the governorship in 1876, but lost the race. By 1880, he was elected to the U.S. Senate.

As senator, Harrison became an outspoken critic of President Cleveland. He supported important legislation such as civil service reform and railroad regulation. In 1888, the Republican Party chose Harrison to run against Cleveland. The Harrison name proved an asset to the party in that election. The key issue was tariffs; Harrison wanted them higher and Cleveland wanted them lower. Harrison defeated Cleveland by a 90,000 vote majority. (The campaign waged by the Republicans was probably one of the most corrupt in American history, but Harrison was not aware of the fact.)

The Presidency of Benjamin Harrison

Once president, Harrison enjoyed Republican majorities in both houses of Congress for his first two years in office.

Harrison continued to fight for civil service reform, adding 11,000 offices to the list of classified government jobs filled through civil service exams.

The Harrison administration witnessed an increase in the number of states in the Union. Six western territories gained statehood: North and South Dakota, Montana, Wyoming, Idaho, and Washington. The territory of Oklahoma was created out of the land given to Native Americans earlier in the 19th century through a Congressional act called the Organic Act.

Congress passed an important piece of legislation with Harrison's support. The Sherman Antitrust Act made monopolistic business practices illegal. In addition, Congress passed a higher tariff bill—a goal of Harrison's—called the McKinley Tariff Act. The act was designed to protect American businesses and manufacturers. But the new law caused higher prices in the United States and contributed to the depression of 1893.

In foreign policy, the Harrison administration pursued increased trade with foreign nations. Also, the United States called for the first conference of nations in the Western Hemisphere—the Pan American Conference, in 1889.

Harrison faced possible annexation of Hawaii during his presidency. In 1893, the Hawaiian queen was overthrown through a revolution backed and financed by American planters and businessmen on the islands. By year's end, the islands requested territorial status with the United States and the Harrison administration negotiated a treaty to be approved by the Senate. Harrison's term ended before the treaty was ratified and President Cleveland refused to pursue its ratification, feeling the revolution had been manipulated by greedy American businessmen.

The Harrisons enjoyed life in the White House and saw new innovations introduced there, such as the installation of electric lights. But they rarely used them for fear of electric shock. They continued to rely on gas lights.

Harrison ran for re-election in 1892, but lost to Grover Cleveland. Traditional voters for the Republican Party, including farmers, abandoned the Republicans and supported a third party candidate, James B. Weaver, who ran for the newly created Populist Party. Factory workers also voted Populist instead of Republican, since Harrison's administration had responded negatively to labor unrest during his term. Cleveland received approximately 300,000 more votes than Harrison.

Following the election, Harrison returned to his legal practice in Indianapolis. (Sadly, his wife died just two weeks before the election.) He later remarried his wife's nurse, Mrs. Dimmick. The couple produced one child named Elizabeth. In his retirement, Harrison wrote and published. His role in later politics was limited, but he did help negotiate a treaty with Great Britain on behalf of Venezuela. Harrison died on March 13, 1901.

Review and Write

1. How did Benjamin Harrison's ancestors make their contribution to American history?

2. What traditional Republican groups defected and voted for the Populist Party in 1892, and why?

William McKinley

1897–1901

The Rise of William McKinley

To some people he seemed warm and charming; to others, pretentious and cool. A highly moral, and religious man, McKinley was known for his kindness, especially to his wife, an invalid and epileptic. But during his presidency, the United States engaged in a calculating war in Cuba, and a bloody struggle over American control of the Philippines.

On January 29, 1843, William McKinley was born in his family's home which doubled as a country store in the small town of Niles, Ohio. His family had moved to America from Ireland a century before his birth. One of nine children born to William and Nancy Allison McKinley, young William attended Poland Seminary, a private school. At 17, he attended Allegheny College, but did not graduate due to illness.

He volunteered for duty in the Civil War in 1861 and served under future president, Rutherford B. Hayes. He saw action at the battle of Antietam. McKinley was cited for bravery for his actions during the daylong battle and received a promotion. Following the war, he studied law and was admitted to the bar in 1867. He soon took up practice in Canton, Ohio.

Always interested in politics, he was elected prosecuting attorney of Stark County, Ohio, in 1869. Two years later, he married Ida Saxton, the daughter of a local newspaper publisher. The couple had two children, one of whom died at four months. Mrs. McKinley became ill afterwards and for the remainder of her life, McKinley looked after his wife with great care. (She later developed epilepsy.) Everyone who knew the McKinleys thought of William as one of the kindest of husbands.

Through the 1870s and 1880s, William McKinley expanded his political role, and was elected to the U.S. House of Representatives in 1876 where he served until 1891. In the House, he supported high tariffs, one of which was named for him. He also supported the expanded circulation of silver coinage over gold.

After facing defeat in the House in 1890, McKinley went on to be elected governor of Ohio in 1891. His popularity and influence brought him national attention. In 1892, members of the Republican Party attempted to nominate him as the party's candidate, but failed. An 1896 effort was more successful, and McKinley ran against William Jennings Bryan from Nebraska.

McKinley's "front porch" campaign—one typical in that day—was different from Bryan's strategy of crisscrossing the country by train and speaking to hundreds of thousands of people. In part, McKinley refused to stump across the country in 1896 because of his wife's physical condition. He refused to leave her alone. Instead of the candidate touring the country, the voters went to McKinley.

The Presidency of William McKinley

With McKinley staying at home, the Republicans spent $3.5 million on McKinley's election compared to $300,000 for Bryan. McKinley's campaign manager was a wealthy businessman from Ohio, Mark Hanna. Hanna orchestrated opportunities for voters to travel to McKinley's home in Canton where they could hear the candidate deliver speeches from his own front porch. McKinley won by a 600,000-vote majority.

McKinley's presidency was one of great economic growth and extraordinary development in foreign affairs. (The country was just emerging from a depression in 1897.) To protect domestic manufacturing, McKinley supported higher tariffs. He altered his earlier commitment to expanded silver coinage by supporting the Gold Standard Act of 1900.

But nothing marked the McKinley presidency more than the Spanish-American War of 1898. For a year, McKinley avoided going to war with Spain over Spain's domination of Cuba. As more and more Americans supported U.S. intervention, McKinley finally succumbed to pressure and asked Congress to declare war.

The conflict lasted only a few months, yet America emerged from the war with control of Puerto Rico, Cuba, and the Philippines. (Other events brought Guam, Hawaii, and Samoa under American domination.) McKinley suddenly found himself presiding over a far-flung colonial empire. Such changes brought the United States to the front as a major world power.

McKinley debated long and hard over the annexation of the Philippine Islands by the United States following the Spanish-American War. Unlike Puerto Rico and Cuba, the Philippines were far removed from the United States by thousands of ocean miles. McKinley was not certain of the appropriateness of American control of land such a distance away. But he finally relented.

In retrospect, the American annexation of the Philippines was costly. The Filipino people had supported the United States during the Spanish-American War when independence looked imminent. But they did not desire American control of their islands any more than they wanted a continuation of Spanish control. A costly three-year war developed between Filipino rebels and American troops. Thousands of American soldiers were killed or died of tropical diseases trying to subdue the Filipinos.

In 1900, American prosperity and the victory over the Spanish brought McKinley a second term as president. He again defeated William Jennings Bryan using the slogan, "four more years of the full dinner pail."

But McKinley's second term lasted only a few months before he was assassinated by an anarchist named Leon Czolgosz. Czolgosz shot the president at close range while attending a reception held by McKinley at the Pan-American Exposition in Buffalo, New York. After a nine-day struggle with his bullet wounds, McKinley died on September 14, 1901.

Review and Write

1. How would you describe the personal relationship between McKinley and his wife?

2. In what ways did the United States become a world power during the McKinley administration?

Theodore Roosevelt

1901–1909

The Rise of Theodore Roosevelt

Few men in American politics have brought more personality to the presidency than did Theodore Roosevelt. Thrust into the White House in 1901 following the assassination of President McKinley, Roosevelt, then just 42, was the youngest man to become president.

He was known for his boundless energy and American spirit. An avid outdoorsman, Roosevelt was a hunter, sportsman, hiker, horseman, and boxer. (He lost the use of an eye during a boxing match in later years.) But he was also a scholar, an enthusiastic reader, and the author of several books on American history.

A veteran of the Spanish-American War, President Roosevelt pursued the extension of American interests overseas, increasing America's role as a global policeman. Such an approach to international relations sometimes created hard feelings between the U.S. and some foreign powers. Without doubt, the U.S. emerged from the Roosevelt years as a world leader.

At home, Roosevelt pursued progressive reforms. During his presidency, the government filed suit against numerous corporations in an effort to break up large business monopolies. He encouraged political reform, protective laws, and a national conservation policy. All through his energetic years

as president, he appeared to be having the time of his life. He later said of his presidency, "I do not believe that anyone else has ever enjoyed the White House as much as I have."

Theodore Roosevelt was born on October 27, 1858, in New York City. His parents were Theodore and Martha Bulloch Roosevelt. Theodore was one of four children. The Roosevelts were descended from Dutch immigrants—known as the Van Roosevelts—who had come to America in the 1640s. During the Civil War, Theodore's mother and father supported different sides. (She was from a well-known Georgia family.)

As a youth, Roosevelt was frail, small, and sickly, suffering from asthma. From an early age, he wore eyeglasses. But he developed a love for athletics and the outdoors, as well as reading. His family traveled around the world as young Theodore was growing up, exposing him to the wonders of exotic locales from Europe to the Middle East. Such experiences helped form young Teddy Roosevelt's thirst for knowledge.

After an early education under private tutors, Theodore entered Harvard University in 1876. He met his future wife, Alice Hathaway Lee, during his college years, and married her in 1880. After his graduation, Roosevelt enrolled in Columbia University Law School, but soon dropped out. He turned to politics instead. At age 23, he was elected to the New York state assembly. During these years, he became personal and political friends with then-governor, Grover Cleveland.

The Presidency of Theodore Roosevelt

In 1884, a double tragedy struck. Theodore's wife, Alice, died following childbirth on Valentine's Day. His grief was compounded by his mother's death on the same day.

Suffering from his loss, Theodore left New York and bought two cattle ranches in the Dakota Territory. There he worked as a cowboy by day, and wrote by night. During this period, he helped round up a gang of cattle rustlers, and once punched out a cowboy in a saloon who made fun of his glasses.

By 1886, Roosevelt had given up ranching and remarried, this time to Edith Kermit Carow, an old family friend. The Roosevelts had five children (plus Alice, from Theodore's first marriage).

In 1888, the Republicans once again controlled the presidency. Roosevelt was appointed by President Harrison to serve as a member of the Civil Service Commission, then New York City Police Commissioner, followed by an appointment by McKinley to assistant secretary of the navy.

When war with Spain came in 1898, Roosevelt resigned his post, and organized a group of volunteers for service called the Rough Riders. He and his men—many of them old college classmates, football buddies, and fellow Dakota cowboys—went to fight in Cuba.

Returning from the war, Roosevelt ran for the New York governorship and won. By then, he was a household name. In 1900, he was selected as McKinley's second vice-presidential running mate. Once elected, Roosevelt soon found himself McKinley's successor following the president's death at the hands of an assassin.

Roosevelt began his presidency with a promise to the Republican Party that he would continue following the course begun by President McKinley. But it didn't take long before Roosevelt was unable to stay the course. He had his own identity as the nation's chief executive.

Early in his presidency, Roosevelt promised businessmen and industrialists that he would not attempt to limit their actions in the financial world. But within his first year in office, he began to reign in the excesses of the big trusts. These monopolies soon became a main target of the

The White House

Roosevelt administration.

One of the first corporations to face the Roosevelt challenge was the Northern Securities Company. This well-financed investment firm was one of Wall Street tycoon J.P. Morgan's businesses. The government felt that Northern Securities was guilty of eliminating competition. In 1904, the federal government ordered the dissolution of Northern Securities. During the Roosevelt administration, the federal justice department filed 43 suits against major corporations and alleged monopolies. Such actions gained Theodore Roosevelt the name of "Trust Buster."

Roosevelt also used the power of the federal government to give some support to the struggling labor unions of the period. During a 1902 coal strike, 140,000 members of the United Mine Workers challenged their employers for better pay and improved working conditions. Public opinion was on the side of the miners, but the companies involved refused to negotiate.

The president, with no genuine legal authority to do so, involved himself in the dispute. (The strike had gone on for months, the winter season was approaching, and the nation was facing desperate coal shortages.) He called both the representatives of the union and of the mine owners together and forced them to negotiate. When the mine owners balked at Roosevelt's heavy-handed involvement, he threatened to call out the army and have soldiers occupy and operate the mines. A settlement soon came, with a pay increase for the miners.

Roosevelt also added to his reputation as a conservationist. He added 125 million acres to the national forests and pushed 25 irrigation and land reclamation projects through. A great dam began construction in Arizona, which would later bear his name.

It was during his presidency that the novel, *The Jungle*, by Upton Sinclair, exposed the filthy sanitation conditions of America's meatpacking plants. He pushed Congress to investigate, and supported the Meat Inspection Act, and the Food and Drugs Act.

In foreign policy, President Roosevelt was forceful—even threatening—with some foreign powers. He supported the Monroe Doctrine, which had earlier in the 19th century declared the Western Hemisphere no longer subject to European intervention and colonization. He intervened in 1902 when the South American nation of Venezuela, heavily in debt to Great Britain and Germany, was threatened with a blockade of her ports. He threatened to use military force against the Germans if they did not withdraw their warships from Venezuelan waters. Such interventions into Latin American affairs became known as the "Roosevelt Corollary" to the Monroe Doctrine. Through Roosevelt's efforts, the United States began building the Panama Canal.

His success brought victory in the 1904 election. In 1905, Roosevelt helped negotiate an end to the war between Japan and Russia, with the president serving as mediator. For his efforts, Roosevelt received the Nobel Peace Prize.

At the end of his second term, Roosevelt hand-picked the next Republican candidate—his secretary of war, William Taft. After his retirement, Roosevelt went on hunting trips to Africa and kept a close watch on American politics. When Taft's presidency failed to satisfy Roosevelt, he ran against his old friend in the 1912 election on the Progressive Party ticket. During the campaign, an assassin attempted to kill Roosevelt, shooting him in the chest at close range. Roosevelt survived the wound, but lost the election, not to Taft, but to the Democratic challenger, Woodrow Wilson.

When World War I began, Roosevelt asked to lead a division of troops, but Wilson thought Roosevelt was too old. Theodore Roosevelt died on January 6, 1919.

Review and Write

1. Describe Roosevelt's trust-busting.

2. Theodore Roosevelt was an extremely talented politician. What do you think was his greatest achievement as president of the United States?

William Howard Taft

1909–1913

The Rise of William Howard Taft

Perhaps no one ever wanted to be president of the United States less than William Howard Taft. He wanted, instead, to be a member of the Supreme Court. Even as a child, Taft had a keen legal mind. His mother once said of him, "I do not want my son to be president. His is a judicial mind and he loves the law." During his lifetime of public service, Taft would serve both roles. He did not enjoy his presidency, a role he took on after being spurred to run by his wife. But he relished his later years, following his single term as president, when he was the chief justice of the Supreme Court. No one else has ever held both positions in American history.

As a person, Taft was a genial man. Heavy-set, (weighing 300 pounds), he was seen as warm, kind, and honest. Despite his size, he remained active all his life, enjoying golf, horseback riding, tennis, and walking. He was considered an excellent dancer. But unlike the showy, immodest Roosevelt, Taft was a quiet man who did not enjoy the glare of attention brought by being the chief executive.

He was born in Cincinnati, Ohio, on September 15, 1857. His ancestors had lived in colonial America during the 1600s. His father, Alphonso, was a judge. His mother was Louise Maria Torrey Taft. William was their second son. He had two brothers, two half-brothers, and a sister. Playing together as children, William was called "Big Lub" by his siblings.

He entered Yale at age 17, graduating in 1878. Taft then went to law school in Cincinnati and was admitted to the bar two years later. He served as an assistant prosecuting attorney, and was Cincinnati's collector of internal revenue in 1882. By the late 1880s, Taft was in a successful private law practice.

He married Helen Harron on June 19, 1886. Her father was a lawyer and she proved ambitious enough for both herself and William. The couple had three children, one of whom—Robert—later became a U.S. senator. In 1887, Taft received his first judgeship, serving on the Cincinnati superior court. It was to be one of his few elected offices.

Three years later, President Benjamin Harrison chose Taft as the solicitor general of the U.S. Taft argued over a dozen cases for the government, appearing before the U.S. Supreme Court. He gained another judgeship by appointment in 1892, serving as a circuit judge. During several of the following years, he was dean of the University of Cincinnati Law School.

In 1900, Taft went abroad to serve on a civil commission to govern the Philippine Islands. The next year, he was chosen to be governor. As a colonial official, Taft treated the Filipinos justly, establishing courts, building roads, distributing land to the poor, and helping pave the way for Filipino independence. When an appointment to the U.S. Supreme Court came in 1902, Taft turned it down, believing his mission to the Filipinos was not yet finished.

The Presidency of William Howard Taft

Taft joined Roosevelt's cabinet in 1904 as secretary of war. Roosevelt called on Taft frequently, asking him to establish a U.S.-controlled government in the Panama Canal Zone and to help negotiate an end to the Russo-Japanese War. By 1908, he was Roosevelt's choice for president. Despite his lack of interest in running for president, Mrs. Taft and his brothers convinced him to run.

At the Republican convention, he won the nomination on the first draft. A New York House Representative named James S. Sherman was selected as Taft's vice-presidential running mate. His Democratic challenger was William Jennings Bryan of Nebraska, who had been defeated twice—in 1896 and 1900—for the presidency. Taft defeated him by a margin of over one million votes.

Without a doubt, Mrs. Taft's own personal ambition led her husband to accept the nomination for president in 1808. During their first year in the White House, she relished her role as First Lady and served as hostess at state dinners, receptions, and balls. It was through her efforts that the mayor of Japan sent 3000 Japanese cherry trees to America to be planted along the banks of the Potomac River in Washington, D.C. Tragically, however, she suffered a stroke in 1909, which made hosting difficult. For the majority of Taft's presidency, either the Tafts' daughter or the First Lady's sister served as White House hostess.

It took little time for the nation to discover that mild-mannered Taft was not like the boisterous Theodore Roosevelt. But Taft did achieve some goals as president. He established the Tariff Board to examine tariff rates. While he believed that United States industry needed the protection of tariffs, he favored lowering them significantly. Congress did pass a lower tariff bill during Taft's presidency—the Payne-Aldrich Tariff—but did not reduce tariff rates to any great extent.

Taft also encouraged the establishment of a commerce court and helped strengthen the Interstate Commerce Commission. He actively broke up trusts as had Roosevelt. In fact, twice as many trusts were "busted" by Taft as by Roosevelt and in only one presidential term.

In foreign policy, the Taft administration accumulated an uneven record. He encouraged "dollar diplomacy" by which the U.S. government made loans to several Latin American nations and China to encourage investment by American banks and businesses in those regional markets. The policy generally failed.

Perhaps Taft's greatest mistake as president was to fire his chief forester, Gifford Pinchot, who was critical of Taft's secretary of the interior. When he fired Pinchot, he drew the anger of Roosevelt who decided to run against Taft in the 1912 election.

Both men lost the campaign to Woodrow Wilson. Following his presidency, Taft taught constitutional law at Yale University. In 1921, his dream of a Supreme Court seat became reality when President Warren Harding appointed him as chief justice.

While on the Court, he served as a responsible administrator and helped achieve passage of the Judiciary Act, which helped streamline the Court's actions. He also saw through Congress's plans for the building of a new Supreme Court building. He died March 8, 1930, of heart problems, and was buried in Arlington National Cemetery.

Review and Write

In what ways was Taft different from Theodore Roosevelt?

_____

_____

_____

_____

Woodrow Wilson

1913–1921

The Rise of Woodrow Wilson

Woodrow Wilson is considered one of the most successful presidents in American history. All the qualities Americans admire —honesty, integrity, perseverance, moral character, readiness to stand up for what is right—were significant aspects of Wilson's personality. And he brought them all to his role as president.

He presided over the country at a time of great upheaval. The nation was becoming increasingly modern and expansive. It was also a time of war, and Wilson took the American people into World War I—an extremely bloody conflict. But America emerged victorious from that war, and was ever after recognized as one of the leading world powers of the modern era.

He was the third of four children born to Joseph Ruggles Wilson and Janet Woodrow Wilson, in Staunton, Virginia, on December 29, 1856. Joseph Wilson was a Presbyterian minister and Woodrow's mother was a minister's daughter. Young Woodrow was raised with a keen sense of morality and grew up to be a religious man. At age two, Woodrow's family moved to Georgia. As a child, Wilson recalled memories of General Sherman's march through Georgia and the death of Abraham Lincoln.

He did not begin attending school until after the Civil War. He studied with his father and, at age 17, entered Davidson College in North Carolina. In his second year of studies, he began attending Princeton University (then called the College of New Jersey). He graduated from Princeton in 1879 and immediately entered law school in Virginia. Three years later, he opened a law office in Atlanta but did not receive many clients. He left the practice in 1883, and began graduate studies in history and political science at Johns Hopkins University in Baltimore. That year, he met Ellen Axson. Like Wilson's mother, Ellen was the daughter of a Presbyterian minister. They married in 1885, and over the years had three daughters.

Wilson proved to be a brilliant student. He published a book on politics in 1885 that was highly praised. He completed his doctoral studies in the summer of 1886, and received his Ph.D. Through the end of the decade, Wilson served as a history and political science professor at several colleges and universities, including Bryn Mawr— a women's college.

While teaching at Wesleyan University in Connecticut, Wilson coached a successful university football team. He continued his scholastic studies, writing and publishing political science textbooks. In 1890, he was asked to serve on the faculty at Princeton.

While teaching at Princeton, Wilson solidified his reputation as a scholar and soon became one of the most popular professors at the university.

The Road to the White House

In 1902, Wilson was offered the presidency of Princeton University, chosen unanimously by the institution's trustees. He was the first nonclergyman to be Princeton's president.

Wilson applied the same level of academics to administrating the university as he did as a history professor. His attempts to reform the university's curriculum and change the college student club structure caused him criticism from the university's tradition-minded alumni. But his work at Princeton gained Wilson a statewide, even national reputation as a man of honesty, integrity, and scholarly ingenuity.

By 1910, party officials in New Jersey began to consider Wilson for the state governorship. By then, ready for a change, on October 20, 1910, he resigned the presidency of Princeton to run for governor. His speeches won him many supporters as he spoke for the need for reform at a state level. He received more votes for governor than any Democrat had ever won in New Jersey to that date.

As governor, Wilson pushed for a long list of statewide reforms. The state legislature supported such Wilson proposals as a primary election law, an employers' liability act, school reform, and a law regulating public utilities. In little more than a year as governor, Wilson was already being noticed as a progressive reformer. That wing of the Democratic Party, in 1911, approached Wilson to run as the Party's nominee for the U.S. presidency. But the stage for the presidency was a crowded one. Wilson faced two major opponents in 1912— President William Taft, and former president, Theodore Roosevelt.

Two factors worked together to ensure the election of Woodrow Wilson as president in 1912—his personal and political reputation, and the division of Republican support between President Taft and the Progressive Party candidate, former President Theodore Roosevelt, a longtime Republican. His electoral votes tallied 435, while Roosevelt and Taft combined accumulated fewer than 100 votes.

Wilson took to the presidency with vigor and resolve. Soon he was at work on tariff issues, banking questions, and business problems. Within his first two weeks in office, he held his first press conference to keep the people informed.

A month into his presidency, Wilson appeared before Congress to explain his political goals. (No president had done so since John Adams.) His tariff proposal passed easily through Congress. Called the Underwood Tariff Act, it lowered import rates and eliminated tariffs on such items as steel rails, sugar, and wool.

Encouraged by this success, Wilson introduced a new concept for the federal banking system. His agenda included the establishment of 12 reserve banks under the directorship of a Federal Reserve Board. It was a controversial move, and Congress debated the plan for six months before agreeing to it in much the same form as Wilson had introduced it.

Other reforms passed through Congress at Wilson's suggestion. The Federal Trade Commission was established. A new antitrust act was passed. Labor legislation went into law, including an eight- hour work day for railroad workers, and a Child Labor Act which limited the number of hours a child could work. Rural school systems received more money. Taxes were increased for wealthier Americans. Most of Wilson's domestic agenda was passed by Congress during his first term in office.

The Fourteen Point Dream

Wilson faced greater challenges in his foreign policy. Throughout his entire administration, the United States and Mexico were at odds. A new dictator, Victoriano Huerta, came to power in Mexico in 1913, and Wilson encouraged Mexican revolutionaries to buy guns to use against the Huerta regime. When some drunken American sailors were arrested by Huerta officials in Veracruz, in 1914, Wilson demanded an apology from the Mexican leader. Huerta refused, and Wilson ordered U.S. forces to occupy Veracruz. The action resulted in poorer relations with Mexico plus 18 American deaths.

Wilson was plagued by other Mexican problems such as raids into American New Mexico by a revolutionary named Pancho Villa. In response to the raids, Wilson sent an expedition of army forces to Mexico to catch Villa. They never caught up with him.

But Wilson's greatest foreign challenge was World War I. When war began in July of 1914, with Germany and its ally Austria-Hungary facing Britain, France, and Russia, Wilson was determined to keep America out of the conflict. By 1916, he was able to campaign for re-election with the slogan, "He kept us out of war."

As Wilson grappled with keeping America neutral, personal tragedy struck. His wife died on August 6, 1914. Deeply saddened, Wilson grieved until he met Edith Galt, a Washington widow. They married in late 1915.

As Germany became more aggressive, and sank American merchant vessels, Wilson could no longer restrain himself or the American people. By April 1917, he went to Congress to ask for a declaration of war against Germany.

As a wartime leader, Wilson gained the enthusiastic support of the American people. U.S. involvement came at a crucial time in the conflict, and the Allies, by 1918, were able to defeat the Germans and their cobelligerents. But long before the war was over, Wilson was looking ahead. In January of 1918, he presented to the U.S. Congress his plan for peace and security in the postwar world called the "Fourteen Point Plan." By eliminating the causes of world war—such as secret diplomacy, violations of sea rights, and arms build-up—Wilson hoped to make the Great War the last one in history.

During the peace negotiations, Wilson presented the conference with his Fourteen Point Plan for world peace, which included the forming of an international organization called the League of Nations. Yet the U.S. Senate rejected Wilson's plan, and never signed the Versailles Treaty or joined the League. When rejection seemed clear in the summer of 1919, Wilson took his cause to the American people, traveling across the country, speaking in dozens of cities and towns, trying to regain his dream. Finally, exhausted from his wartime efforts,

Wilson suffered a stroke in late 1919.

The final year of Wilson's presidency was shrouded in controversy. Unable to speak or even write much of the time, Wilson's wife, Edith, kept him in virtual seclusion, often refusing to allow even cabinet members to see the president. Sometimes she would carry documents into her husband's sick room, and emerge with them signed in a questionable handwriting. Although he appeared unable to carry out his duties as president, Edith shielded him from the public.

In 1920, Wilson was awarded the Nobel Peace Prize and spent his retirement quietly. He never fully recovered from his stroke and died in his sleep on February 3, 1924.

Review and Write

How did Wilson gain the attention of the American people prior to his presidency?

_____

_____

_____

_____

_____

_____

_____

_____

_____

_____

Warren G. Harding

1921–1923

The Rise of Warren G. Harding

Warren Gamaliel Harding was the first American president elected with the full participation of women voters. The 19th Amendment to the U.S. Constitution was ratified in August of 1920, just in time to help Harding— a handsome and distinguished senator from Ohio—get elected as America's 29th president.

Americans voted for Harding because they wanted a change. Many citizens were tired of progressive legislation and U.S. involvement in the bloody conflict of World War I—a war that took over 100,000 American lives. Some Americans felt the country had not gained enough from U.S. involvement in the conflict and many were unprepared to watch America assume the position of world leader.

Harding promised change for America. He spoke of "returning to normalcy," a call which most Americans interpreted as a return to a life that was simpler—to life before war, and before the endless campaigns for social and moral reform. Harding was a man of his time, a fun-loving fellow who liked his bootleg whiskey, poker, and a good cigar. It was the decade of the "Roaring 20s," and Harding fit in just perfectly.

He was born on November 2, 1865, on a farm outside Blooming Grove, Ohio. Warren Harding was the son of George Tryon Harding and Phoebe Dickerson Harding. The family descended from early Puritan settlers who had come to America in 1624. Young Warren was the oldest of the Harding's eight children.

He attended public school in rural Ohio and worked part-time as a typesetter for a local newspaper. Warren entered college at age 14 and graduated at 17. For the next few years, he taught school, sold insurance, and returned to newspaper work, this time as a writer and editor.

In his mid-20s, Harding married a woman five years older than he named Florence Kling DeWolfe. Known to Warren as "Duchess," Florence—a forceful woman—helped him in his career. Harding by then was part owner in an Ohio weekly called the *Marion Star*. With the help of Duchess, the *Star* became a daily paper. The Hardings had no children.

As Harding's reputation in Ohio grew, he went into politics. He was elected Republican state senator in 1898 and five years later became lieutenant governor. When he ran for the governorship in 1910, he lost.

Through his involvement in Republican national politics, Harding continued his rise to the presidency. He attended Republican caucuses and nominating conventions. He nominated Taft as the Republican candidate at the 1912 convention. In 1916, Harding ran for the U.S. Senate and won.

Harding was well liked in Congress, but was a lackluster senator. Never did he propose a single significant bill. He was frequently absent in the

Senate chamber when votes were taken. He did vote in support of women's voting rights, and more federal control of big business. (He admitted later that the women's suffrage issue had not really been that important to him.) He also gave his support to high tariffs.

The Presidency of Warren G. Harding

When the 1920 Republican convention deadlocked in the dispute over a candidate for the presidency, party leaders met behind closed doors and emerged with a compromise candidate— Warren Harding. His opposition was Democratic candidate and Ohio governor, James Cox, and his running mate, young Franklin Roosevelt.

As with many presidential candidates during this era, Harding did not actively campaign for president himself. Instead, he carried out a typical "front porch" campaign based at his home in Marion, Ohio. As people gathered at his house, he spoke briefly and shook many hands. Harding rarely spoke directly to the issues. He was much more inclined to skirt around an issue by responding vaguely or through unclear promises for the future. He never took a clear stance on the issue of American involvement in the League of Nations, although he had voted against it as a senator.

Harding was elected by a landslide over his Democratic challenger. Several factors distinguish this election from previous ones. First, Harding was the first president ever elected while serving in the U.S. Senate. Since the 19th Amendment went into effect in 1920, this election was the first in which women across the country could vote for president. And for the first time, presidential election returns were broadcast over the radio.

As president, Harding was mediocre. He provided little enthusiastic presidential leadership and often relied on Congress, as well as his cabinet, for ideas and direction. Harding signed a peace treaty finally ending the controversy of Wilson's proposed League of Nations. The treaty did not include American membership in the League.

Harding's greatest flaw as president was his selection of a cabinet. Many of its members became involved in political deals and scandals that further marred the Harding administration. Among those in his administration who found themselves in the midst of scandal were his secretary of the interior, Albert B. Fall. Fall was discovered to have received bribes from oil companies to grant them leases over federally controlled land in the West for the purpose of drilling for oil. The reserves in question included land in Elk Hills, California, and Teapot Dome, Wyoming. Fall was convicted (following the Harding administration) for taking bribes, and was sentenced to a term in prison. He was the first cabinet member in history to be convicted. Another cabinet member, Attorney General Harry M. Daugherty faced charges in 1926 for receiving bribes from Prohibition violators. At least two other Harding bureaucrats committed suicide over scandals in their departments.

But Harding's administration was not all about scandal and bribes. Some of his cabinet members, including his secretary of the treasury, Andrew Mellon, were honest men. Mellon worked hard to cut federal spending and taxes on incomes, corporate profits, and inheritances.

Through it all, President Harding remained popular with the American people. They had voted for a hands-off president, and Harding played the role. Aware of his administration's poor reputation, Harding went on a speaking tour in the summer of 1923 to bolster his image. He died on August 2 while in California. The exact cause of death was never determined.

Review and Write

What was Harding's greatest mistake as president and how significant an error did it prove to be?

_____

_____

_____

_____

_____

Calvin Coolidge

1923–1929

The Rise of Calvin Coolidge

Americans have become accustomed to seeing politicians—especially their president—on television, expressing himself on one issue or another. But Calvin Coolidge was president during another time. He did not present himself daily to as many media forums as possible, but rather spoke little in public, and kept his words to a minimum.

Coolidge was the sixth president in U.S. history to ascend to the White House upon the death of a president. Often overlooked by historians as a poor president, Coolidge managed to make a success of his presidency. But events following Coolidge's presidency sometimes caused his achievements to appear minor or even inadequate. Thus his reputation as president has been marred by the direction of history.

He was born on the 4th of July, 1872, in Plymouth Notch, Vermont. His full name was John Calvin Coolidge (after his father), but the family called him Calvin or Cal. The Coolidge family had lived in colonial New England since 1630. Calvin's mother, Victoria Moor Coolidge, died when he was only 12 years old. He had one sister who died young.

At age 13, young Calvin attended Black River Academy and graduated in 1890. He entered Amherst College the following year, where he honed an interest and involvement in politics. Following graduation from Amherst, he studied law and was admitted to the bar in 1897, then opened up his own law office.

His political career began with an election to city council in 1898, and city attorney in 1900. By 1904, Calvin Coolidge met his future bride, Grace Anna Goodhue, a teacher at a school for the deaf. While Coolidge was shy and quiet, Grace was outgoing and lively. They married on October 4, 1905, and had two children.

Coolidge moved on politically and became involved in state politics. He was elected to the Massachusetts House of Representatives in 1906 and served in the state senate from 1912 to 1915, when he was elected lieutenant governor. In 1918, he was elected governor. As governor he took a strong position against a police strike in 1919 and won national attention. His simple, 15-word reply to the striking policemen won the approval of many Americans. "There is no right to strike against the public safety by anybody, anywhere, any time."

His reputation within the Republican Party solidly in place by 1920, Coolidge was nominated for the vice-presidency on the ticket with presidential candidate, Warren Harding. The two men won a solid victory over the Democratic challenger, James Cox, of Ohio.

Although it had not been customary for vice presidents to do so, Harding requested Coolidge's presence at cabinet meetings. Yet Coolidge said little and kept in the background. But when President

Harding died in the summer of 1923, Coolidge was thrust into the forefront.

The Presidency of Calvin Coolidge

When Coolidge received word of President Harding's death in the summer of 1923, he was on vacation at his father's home. He was awakened late at night and took the oath of office almost immediately. It was administered by his father, who was a notary public. Two weeks later, Coolidge repeated his oath, this time before a Supreme Court justice. Coolidge's attorney general, Harry M. Daugherty, questioned the legality of the oath administered by Coolidge's father.

The scandals of the Harding administration began to break as Coolidge took office. Never implicated in wrongdoing, the president allowed the guilty to be tried and sentenced with little involvement from him. Coolidge spent his time, instead, continuing Harding's conservative economic policies. He helped reduce the national debt by $1 billion during his presidency and called for a reduction of the income tax.

The twenties was a decade of prosperity for many Americans and Coolidge gained political prestige and popularity accordingly. He encouraged growth in the economy and did nothing to limit the speculation in the stock market taking place in the late 1920s.

In 1924, his popularity brought him renomination by his party where he faced no serious challenger. The Democrats selected as their candidate, John W. Davis, who had served as ambassador to Great Britain. A third candidate sprang from the ranks of progressive-minded Republicans and Democrats alike. The Progressive Party nominated Robert M. LaFollette from Wisconsin. LaFollette was a long-standing progressive and had been involved in national politics for 20 years. As the election neared in the fall, the Republicans campaigned for their president with the slogan "Keep Cool with Coolidge." The Democrats touted the Republican scandals of the Harding administration to the voting public, but Coolidge won the election by a margin of 15.7 million to 8.4 million.

Coolidge's nomination and election as president was overshadowed in 1924 by personal tragedy.

Coolidge's son, Calvin, Jr., died of blood poisoning from an infected blister he had developed while playing tennis. The 16-year-old's death came as a shock to the Coolidges. After that loss, Coolidge admitted that the presidency held no importance to him. To add to his family loss, Coolidge's father died two years later during his son's second term.

In foreign affairs, the Coolidge administration signed such treaties as the Kellogg Pact. Otherwise known as the Kellogg-Briand Pact, this momentous international agreement was designed to eliminate war as a means of solving international problems. French foreign minister, Aristide Briand and Coolidge's secretary of state, Frank B. Kellogg, orchestrated the agreement. Initially, the treaty carried the signatures of 15 countries in 1927, and by 1934, 64 nations had signed the agreement. Coolidge also reestablished friendly relations with Mexico.

In 1927, Coolidge announced he did not intend to run again for the presidency, citing the strain of the White House on him and his wife. The Coolidges moved back to their home in Massachusetts. He wrote his memoirs during his retirement and saw them published in 1929. For several years he wrote a regular newspaper column, writing on matters related to American politics, government, international challenges, and economics. Calvin Coolidge died of a heart attack on January 5, 1933. His wife outlived him by 24 years, dying in 1957.

Review and Write

1. What information in this article indicates that Coolidge was a conservative politician?

2. What were some of the highlights of the Coolidge administration?

Herbert Hoover

1929–1933

The Rise of Herbert Hoover

Unlike most American presidents, Herbert Hoover did not rise to the nation's highest office through involvement in local, state, or national politics. He spent his earlier years pursuing a career as a mining engineer, which ultimately made him a millionaire. Only by chance did Hoover become involved in public life, which led him to the White House.

Elected in 1929, Hoover was prepared to lead the nation toward growth and development. But six months after taking office, the United States plunged into one of the worst depressions in American history. Despite other successes as president, Hoover came to be identified as the president of the early depression years.

The first president born west of the Mississippi, on August 10, 1874, Herbert Hoover's childhood home was West Branch, Iowa. His parents, Jesse Clark Hoover, a blacksmith, and Huldah Randall Minthorn Hoover were the parents of three children.

Mrs. Hoover was a Quaker and when Jesse Hoover died in 1880, she supported the family by preaching and working as a seamstress. Herbert lived with several uncles and enjoyed a childhood of outdoor activities including fishing and swimming. He was schooled at Newberg College, a Quaker school.

As a teenager, Herbert became interested in engineering and chose mining as his field of study. At age 17, he enrolled in Stanford University and worked his way through college delivering newspapers and working at a laundry. His summers were filled with trips from California to Arkansas to study mining firsthand.

Hoover met his future bride at Stanford in the geology department. Lou Henry was a banker's daughter and she and Hoover married on February 10, 1899. Lou Hoover was a well-educated and extraordinary woman. In later years, while her husband was president of the United States, she wrote scholarly articles and conducted research projects. The Hoovers had two sons—one went into politics, the other into mining.

Throughout the 1890s, Hoover's mining expertise sent him around the world from Australia to China. (While there, Mrs. Hoover learned to speak Chinese.) By 1908, he had formed his own mining engineering company. Hoover's public career began in 1914 at the beginning of World War I. When he happened to find himself in London that summer, he was asked by U.S. government officials to organize a food relief program for starving Belgians. His efforts helped save thousands of lives.

Upon returning to the States, President Wilson made Hoover head of the U.S. Food Administration, which had the power to set prices and determine production. Still later in the war, Hoover returned to Europe to organize additional food programs across the continent making him internationally known.

The Presidency of Herbert Hoover

In 1920, both the Democratic and Republican parties courted Hoover to be their candidate for president, but he chose not to run. President Harding subsequently chose him as his secretary of commerce, a position he held throughout the Coolidge administration.

In 1928, Hoover announced his candidacy for president. He had served in two presidential cabinets—Harding's and Coolidge's—and was easily accepted by his party on the convention's first ballot. The Democrats found their challenger to Hoover in New Yorker, Alfred E. Smith. Smith was serving as governor. The primary issues of the campaign included the national economy and Prohibition.

Hoover promised the American people a continuation of the booming economy that had dominated America throughout the 1920s. He also campaigned against the repeal of alcohol. Smith, on the other hand, wanted to see Prohibition ended and the 18th Amendment of the Constitution repealed.

On a personal level, Hoover and Smith presented stark contrasts to one another. Hoover always appeared sober and restrained, wearing conservative blue suits. Smith wore loud, checkered suits, and a brown derby. He had a nasal New York voice, brash and gravelly, and could often be seen in public with a cigar. Smith was also Roman Catholic—a concern to many voters.

When the election was held in November, Hoover was elected by a landslide. He won 40 of 48 states and overwhelmed Smith electorally by a margin of 444 to 87 votes. Rarely has any candidate been elected with a greater mandate than Herbert Hoover.

Between his election and his inauguration, Hoover went to work, making a trip through Latin America to bolster good relations. As president, he took definite steps to create a positive agenda for himself. He helped farmers by supporting the Agricultural Marketing Act. Hoover added three

million acres to the nation's park system. He encouraged a higher tariff—the Smoot-Hawley Tariff—but its high rates helped cause the Great Depression by limiting foreign purchases of U.S. goods.

In 1929, the economy collapsed and continued to spiral out of control throughout the Hoover years. By 1932, 10 million Americans were out of work. Unemployed people erected improvised shacks and lived in depressed areas outside of towns known as Hoovervilles. Hoover's name would forever be linked with the Depression. Hoover ordered little government response to the Depression, assuring people that it would not last. He believed that private enterprise would bring an end to the Depression.

Hoover lost the 1932 election to Franklin Roosevelt. He spent his later years explaining why the Depression had taken place and donating to charities. Hoover wrote and published his memoirs in three volumes. The final volume was not completed until 1961.

In the early 1960s, Hoover served as a trustee for nine private institutions including charities. All the money he received from government pensions, he gave to charity. He lived longer after his presidency than any other chief executive before him, dying on October 20, 1964, at the age of 90.

Review and Write

1. Hoover was a wealthy businessman before his presidency. How had he made his fortune?

_____

_____

_____

2. Hoover's public work began in an almost accidental fashion. How?

_____

_____

_____

Test III

Part I.

Multiple Choice.

Match the information at the left to the answers on the right. Place the letter of the correct answer in the spaces below.

1. Was the only president elected to two nonconsecutive terms.
2. He was assassinated by Charles Guiteau.
3. He was elected after a decision by an electoral commission.
4. Worked on a ranch in the Dakotas raising cattle.
5. Encouraged the flying of the American flag on government buildings.
6. Was assassinated at the Pan American Exposition in Buffalo, New York.
7. This president ended Reconstruction.
8. Was accused of fathering an illegitimate child, which proved to be true.
9. He was diagnosed with a fatal kidney disease during his presidency.
10. His great-grandfather signed the Declaration of Independence.
11. Raised the Rough Riders to fight in the Spanish-American War.
12. In his early years, he was a Disciples of Christ minister.

A. Theodore Roosevelt
B. James Garfield
C. Benjamin Harrison
D. Chester Arthur
E. William McKinley
F. Grover Cleveland
G. Rutherford B. Hayes

Answers:

1. ____ 2. ____ 3. ____ 4. ____ 5. ____ 6. ____ 7. ____ 8. ____ 9. ____ 10. ____ 11. ____ 12. ____

Part II.

Multiple Choice.

Match the information at the left to the answers on the right. Place the letter of the correct answer in the spaces below.

1. Had Congress declare war on Germany.
2. Was famous for his silence and minimum speech.
3. Was a newspaper man from Ohio.
4. Served on the Supreme Court after his presidency.
5. His administration negotiated the Kellogg-Briand Pact.
6. Died in California during his presidency.
7. Was raised by Quaker parents.
8. Was president of Princeton University.
9. Served as governor of Massachusetts.
10. He and his wife were both children of Presbyterian ministers.
11. The Great Depression began during his administration.
12. Was a territorial governor of the Philippines.

A. Herbert Hoover
B. Calvin Coolidge
C. William Taft
D. Warren Harding
E. Woodrow Wilson

Answers:

1. ____ 2. ____ 3. ____ 4. ____ 5. ____ 6. ____ 7. ____ 8. ____ 9. ____ 10. ____ 11. ____ 12. ____

Franklin D. Roosevelt

1933–1945

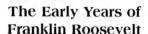

The Early Years of Franklin Roosevelt

Due to an act of Congress, no American will ever serve as president longer than did Franklin Delano Roosevelt. He was first elected in 1932, in the midst of the Great Depression. The American people elected him to three additional, consecutive terms. Had he not died in 1945, FDR would have served until 1949, a total of 16 years as president.

No American president has served during darker days than Roosevelt, with the possible exception of Abraham Lincoln. The two great catastrophes of the American 20th century—the Great Depression and World War II—occurred during the span of the Roosevelt years.

Roosevelt fought both battles with courage, determination, and a cheerful hope for the future. Many of his decisions were controversial then and remain so today, more than a half century after his death. His course of action through his dozen years as chief executive helped to redefine the power of the American presidency, both at home and abroad. From the ashes of World War II, the United States, through FDR's leadership, emerged as one of the world's superpowers.

Just as his distant fifth cousin Theodore, Franklin Roosevelt was born of Dutch ancestry in New York. His birth date was January 30, 1882; the place was his father's family estate at Hyde Park. Franklin was the only child of James and Sara Roosevelt.

Franklin grew up in the Roosevelt household amid wealth and social status. His mother taught him at home and the family made frequent trips to Europe which broadened Franklin's realm of experience. He attended mostly private schools. In 1900, he enrolled at Harvard University and majored in history. He was not an exceptional student and typically received the "Gentleman's C". After graduating, he went to Columbia University Law School and passed the bar in 1907.

During his Harvard years, Franklin began courting a distant cousin, Eleanor Roosevelt. They made plans to marry and did so in 1905. President Theodore Roosevelt, Eleanor's uncle, gave the bride away at the wedding. The Roosevelts had six children, two of whom later served in the U.S. House of Representatives. Franklin enjoyed his children and frequently played with them, taking them sailing in summer and sledding in winter.

In 1910, FDR began his political career with an election to the New York senate. He was 29 years old. After supporting Woodrow Wilson for president in 1912 (over cousin Theodore), Wilson appointed Roosevelt assistant secretary of the navy, a post once held by Teddy Roosevelt. The next year, Roosevelt lost a bid for the U.S. Senate.

During World War I, Roosevelt remained in government service, organizing such wartime projects as the mining of the North Sea. His work in Europe helped give him a national reputation in the press.

The Presidency of Franklin D. Roosevelt

Through his government service during World War I, Franklin Roosevelt was so well known in America that in 1920, the Democrats chose FDR as the vice presidential running mate of presidential candidate James M. Cox of Ohio. Roosevelt and Cox lost the election to Harding and Coolidge.

The loss was a small one to Franklin's career. He moved on and took a vice-presidency in a financial firm, instead. But in 1921, Roosevelt and his family faced a personal tragedy. On August 9, FDR became sick and, within days, was partially paralyzed. He had contracted polio, a crippling muscle disease. Some thought Roosevelt's political future was over.

With determination and a cheerful fortitude in the face of pain, FDR fought back. He exercised and swam often. He visited the therapeutic waters of Warm Springs, Georgia. In time, he built up the strength in his arms and chest, but he never walked again without help.

His political career was far from over, however. In 1924, he attended the Democratic convention and nominated New York Governor Alfred Smith as the candidate. Four years later, FDR was elected governor of New York. In this role, he supported progressive issues and established a relief program for victims of the Great Depression. He was re-elected in 1930.

By 1932, his work as governor had gained him enough national attention for FDR to become the Democratic Party's candidate for president. He campaigned hard, announcing to the American people the need for a "New Deal" for the country. He won, and Americans soon found a friend in the White House.

Inauguration Day 1933 marked the beginning of 12 years of the Roosevelt presidency. Many people in America were anxious about their future and the future of the country. Millions of Americans were unemployed. Thousands of businesses and factories had closed, as well as thousands of banks and lending institutions. The American people were pinning their hope for the future on Franklin Delano Roosevelt. Roosevelt's inaugural speech is remembered as one of hope and optimism. He assured the people of the United States that "the only thing we have to fear is fear itself." His goal was to instill confidence in the American people regarding the future of the economy.

He went to work that day, refusing to attend the Inaugural Ball, insisting there was much work to be done. Roosevelt began gathering around him men and women who could help bring answers to the problems of the Great Depression. Such experts included politicians, teachers, professors, businessmen, and economists. A newspaperman referred to such advisors as the "Brain Trust." Among Roosevelt's advisors, Frances Perkins was the first woman cabinet

Franklin D. Roosevelt's home, "Hyde Park"

member ever. Soon the FDR administration was pressing Congress to enact legislation to solve many of the issues of the Depression.

Roosevelt's first "Hundred Days" in office involved sweeping legislation. By June 16, Congress had enacted important Depression-related bills such as the Agricultural Adjustment Act (AAA), the Tennessee Valley Authority Act (TVA), and the National Industrial Recovery Act (NIRA). Such acts were designed to handle farming crises, labor and industrial problems, and regional economic problems.

Franklin D. Roosevelt's "Hundred Days"

FDR's "Hundred Days" comprised the groundwork for FDR's program known as the New Deal. Other important acts included the Federal Emergency Relief Administration (FERA), which provided states with money for direct relief to struggling families and individuals. The Civilian Conservation Corps (CCC) was established to provide outdoor jobs for America's young men.

By 1935, the Public Works Administration (PWA) was providing billions for the creation of jobs for unemployed workers. Through PWA, federal roads, bridges, dams, and government buildings were constructed. A follow-up act, WPA (Works Progress Administration), passed in 1935, provided jobs for additional millions of people between 1935 and 1942. WPA projects included commissioning artwork to adorn new and old government buildings, as well as employment for musicians, actors, and various other artists.

Although these acts and other FDR legislation did not end the Depression prior to World War II, they did help provide some relief for unemployed and desperate Americans. Some of the acts continued long after the Depression ended, such as Social Security (1935) and the Federal Deposit Insurance Corporation (FDIC) which today protects bank deposits.

Throughout the 1930s, as FDR wrestled with the problems of the Great Depression, he viewed with a watchful eye the dark events in Europe, which ultimately brought the world to war. The rise of dictators in Europe such as Adolf Hitler in Germany and Benito Mussolini in Italy, as well as

the warlords of Japan, created an international coalition of fascists who ultimately instigated the events of World War II.

As Germany, Italy, and Japan attacked their neighboring nations, Roosevelt attempted to maintain America's neutrality. But as the 1930s wore on, he found himself in spiritual alliance with western European powers, such as England and France, as well as China, against the aggressive fascists. When the Japanese launched a surprise attack against American naval and army forces stationed at Pearl Harbor, Hawaii, on December 7, 1941, FDR asked Congress for a declaration of war. Soon, America was in combat with Germany, Italy, and Japan.

The war years—from 1941 to 1945—were difficult for the president and the nation. The conflict involved international strategies and international conferences which taxed Roosevelt greatly. The burden of war preoccupied him constantly. By the spring of 1945, the United States and her Allies were on the verge of defeating Germany. But Franklin D. Roosevelt died on April 12 of a cerebral hemorrhage in Warm Springs, Georgia. America mourned the passing of a great president who had led his countrymen through difficult challenges.

Review and Write

1. What political offices did FDR hold before becoming president of the United States?

2. What was the "Hundred Days" and what was its purpose?

3. Why were the years 1941 to 1945 such a burden to President Roosevelt?

Harry S. Truman

1945–1953

The Rise of Harry S. Truman

Harry S. Truman, vice president from Missouri, inherited the presidency following Roosevelt's death at a difficult time in American history. World War II was not yet over, and Truman had to bring closure to that great international catastrophe. Complicating the end of the war was the beginning of another international conflict. During World War II, the United States' allies included the Soviet Union, a communist-controlled empire that had been attacked by Hitler's Nazi Germany.

Once the Allied powers defeated Germany, the alliance between the United States, England, France, and the Soviet Union began to fall apart. The Soviet Union began to systematically take control of eastern European nations, attempting to install pro-communist governments. Truman soon found himself having to deal with the aggression of the Soviet leader, Josef Stalin, in a postwar confrontation (the cold war), which continued for the next forty years.

The only president to date from Missouri, Harry S. Truman, was born on May 8, 1884, in Lamar, located in the southwestern corner of the state. His parents were John Anderson Truman and Martha Young Truman. Harry was the youngest of three children. (Incidentally, the "S" in his name did not stand for any specific name.)

As a youngster, Harry attended public school after his parents moved to Grandview, then later to Independence, Missouri. He was a voracious reader and claimed to have read by age 14 "all the books in the Independence Public Library." His vision was poor, and he wore glasses from age eight, which kept him out of West Point Military Academy, where he wanted to attend.

As a young man, he worked on railroads, in the Kansas City Star's mailroom, and as a bank bookkeeper. In 1917, he fought in France during the First World War. After returning from the war, he married his longtime girlfriend, Elizabeth "Bess" Wallace. They had first met in a Baptist Sunday School class as children. The Trumans had one daughter, Margaret.

After Truman opened a men's clothing store in 1919 which failed, he moved into politics. He was elected as a county judge in 1922. Other judgeships followed. By 1934, he was elected to the U.S. Senate and was re-elected in 1940, having a reputation for honesty and integrity in office. By 1944, the Democratic Party selected Truman as FDR's third vice president, certain that Roosevelt would not serve out his fourth term due to poor health.

Such a prediction proved true. Five weeks into his fourth term, FDR died on April 12, 1945. His death catapulted Truman into the White House. He then directed the final weeks of war with Germany, seeing Hitler's defeat in early May. (Truman proclaimed May 8—the day marking the Allied victory in

Europe—V-E Day. It was also his birthday.) Within the first two weeks of his presidency, the United Nations met for the first time in San Francisco.

The Presidency of Harry S. Truman

The San Francisco Conference began the long, distinguished history of the United Nations. At the conference, the leaders of dozens of countries met to iron out a plan for an international organization designed to maintain peace in the world and to bring security and progress to both industrial and developing nations. Truman gave his whole-hearted support to the organization and attended the San Francisco Conference.

During the summer of 1945, Truman met with other Allied leaders, including Winston Churchill (who was voted out of office during the conference and replaced by Prime Minister Clement Attlee) and Josef Stalin at Potsdam, Germany. They discussed issues concerning the rebuilding of postwar Europe and the pending defeat of Japan. The discussions were at times awkward and inconclusive, as a rift developed between Truman and Stalin. Truman did not trust Stalin and often took a hard stance against the Soviets. Their personal rivalry and the differences existing between the democratic nations and the communist Soviet Union led to the development of the cold war. It was during the San Francisco Conference that Truman learned of the successful testing of the world's first atomic bomb in the deserts of New Mexico.

By September, the war with Japan was over, but not until Truman detonated an atomic bomb on the Japanese to hasten their surrender. Truman was much criticized for his use of atomic weapons, but he felt the number of American lives saved justified his decision.

Following the conclusion of the Pacific war, Truman's presidency focused on rebuilding Europe and Japan after World War II. In 1947, his Marshall Plan provided U.S. aid to Europe, which brought renewed stability to the West. He consistently stood firm against communism and its aggression around the world in places such as Greece, Turkey, Eastern Europe, and Korea. When the Soviets attempted to block westerners from West Berlin—Germany's divided capital—Truman ordered the Berlin airlift.

In 1948, Truman faced re-election. His party was deeply divided over several issues—especially race. When the Democratic Party platform included a strong civil rights agenda, southern delegates walked out and nominated their own "Dixiecrat" candidate, Strom Thurmond, of South Carolina. Progressive Democrats also bolted from the party and supported former Vice President Henry Wallace. The Republicans nominated New Yorker, Thomas Dewey. Despite the predictions, however, Truman narrowly won the election, taking 28 states.

He challenged Josef Stalin at every turn, causing a widening of the rift between western and communist powers. His support of nationalist forces in China did not stop the communists from taking control there in 1949, however. But when North Korean communist troops invaded pro-Western South Korea in 1950, Truman rushed American forces and United Nations support to help regain South Korea.

Domestically, Truman struggled with a poor postwar economy and labor problems. Otherwise, his "Fair Deal" oversaw increases in social security programs and additional protections for minorities. After his presidency, Truman retired to Missouri, spending his days writing and staying involved in politics. He died December 26, 1972.

Review and Write

Truman took a hard stance against communism during his presidency. What were some of the ways he challenged the spread of communism?

_____

_____

_____

_____

_____

Dwight D. Eisenhower

1953–1961

The Rise of Dwight D. Eisenhower

His career extended from the battlefield to the university campus to the presidency. Before he became chief executive, Dwight D. Eisenhower was a general. During World War II, he became the United States army chief of staff. His leadership and military strategies helped win the war for the Allies and catapulted him to the center of the world stage.

Eisenhower, a hero of World War II, was eventually to rise to the office of the president of the United States. The former general was to become the first Republican president in two decades. He was not the first to become president following a successful military career. Washington, Jackson, and Grant had also risen to political power in just such a manner.

Eisenhower's military experience helped him during his presidency. He was a skilled negotiator who enjoyed a rapport with many of the world's leaders. Yet he could be confrontational in the face of communist aggression from Africa to Latin America. The 1950s was a decade of great social change and economic expansion. Serving through two complete terms, Eisenhower became the oldest president to date.

Dwight David Eisenhower was born on October 14, 1890, a native of Denison, Texas. He was one of seven sons born to David Jacob Eisenhower and Elizabeth Stover Eisenhower. Although Eisenhower became a military figure, he was raised in the Church of the Brethren in Christ, a pacifist sect.

At the age of two, Eisenhower's family moved to Abilene, Kansas, where he grew up on a farm. (His father worked in a creamery.) He attended public school through his adolescent years.

After high school, he applied for a position as a cadet at West Point Military Academy. He did so without his pacifist parents' approval. Eisenhower was accepted and entered West Point in June 1911. Once graduated, Eisenhower was stationed in Texas where he met his future bride, Mamie Geneva Doud. They married on July 1, 1916. They had two sons.

During World War I, Eisenhower trained soldiers for tank duty. For a time, he was stationed in the Panama Canal Zone. He graduated from the Army War College in 1928. During the 1930s, he served as an aide to General Douglas MacArthur in the Philippines.

In 1941, the year the U.S. entered World War II, Eisenhower was a full colonel. But he quickly advanced in the ranks. After the Japanese attack at Pearl Harbor, he was given the task of organizing and planning an Allied invasion of Europe. He helped plan the Allied invasion of North Africa, as well. In the summer of 1942, he was promoted to lieutenant general.

After the success of the Allied invasion in June of 1944, he was promoted to General of the Army.

He served through the remainder of the war and retired from active duty in 1948. Eisenhower was soon appointed president of Columbia University. In 1950, he was appointed supreme commander of NATO forces.

The Presidency of Dwight D. Eisenhower

From the end of World War II, the idea of Eisenhower for president had been supported in various political circles. In 1948, both the Democratic and Republican Parties offered the nomination to the famous general, but he explained that he was a professional soldier, one not connected politically to either party.

But politicians continued to court Eisenhower. In 1952, the Republicans approached him to run for the presidency, and this time he agreed. His running mate was Richard Nixon of California.

In 1952, Eisenhower faced Democratic challenger, Adlai Stevenson, of Illinois. The campaign was a spirited one. Eisenhower was critical of President Truman, especially his conduct in the Korean conflict. He also ran against the Washington establishment, promising to straighten out the nation's messy politics. On election day, Eisenhower defeated Stevenson.

As president, Eisenhower made important and far-reaching decisions that showed his pragmatism and integrity. His cabinet members typically came from business backgrounds, for Eisenhower intended to have the states and private industry help set the political agenda for his administration. Among his cabinet choices was Oveta Culp Hobby, who served as secretary of health, education and welfare, making her the second woman to serve as cabinet department head.

Although Eisenhower was conservative in his social agenda, parts of Roosevelt's New Deal—such as Social Security—were expanded. Eisenhower supported a $1 hike in the minimum wage and favored expansion of welfare to the needy.

He also pushed through Congress a long-range plan for an interstate highway system. The Federal Highway Act of 1956 provided additional growth to the already booming economy of 1950s America.

The act authorized $32 billion for construction of a system of highways across the country. Over the following 20 years, over 40,000 miles of highway were built in America, costing over $75 billion.

Eisenhower endorsed reducing the size of the federal government and turning over some federal power to the states. During his presidency, America began its involvement in space. Following the Soviet launching of the first manmade satellite, Sputnik, in 1957, the United States sent up its first satellite, Explorer I, four months later. In the summer of 1958, Congress, with Eisenhower's endorsement, authorized the creation of the National Aeronautics and Space Administration (NASA).

During the Eisenhower administration, strides were made toward greater civil rights for America's minorities. But Eisenhower's role was very limited in those efforts. He did not support the *Brown v. Topeka* decision that began desegregating public schools. In 1957, however, he did send troops to Little Rock, Arkansas, to protect black students being integrated into that southern city's schools.

His defense policy was aggressive, yet he brought an end to the Korean conflict. He fought communism by bolstering America's ties to free countries worldwide. His challenges to the Soviet Union included threatening the use of nuclear weapons. His Eisenhower Doctrine promised military aid to any Middle East nation in its struggle against communism.

In 1961, Eisenhower retired from the presidency, and moved to a farm near Gettysburg, Pennsylvania. Suffering from heart trouble, he died on March 28, 1969.

Review and Write

Eisenhower was first a general, then a president. Which role do you feel he was best suited for?

_____

_____

_____

_____

John F. Kennedy

1961–1963

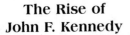

The Rise of John F. Kennedy

While his predecessor in the White House, Dwight Eisenhower, was one of the oldest presidents in American history, John Fitzgerald Kennedy was one of the youngest. A naval veteran of World War II, Kennedy was elected in 1960. His term was cut short by an assassin in November 1963. But he managed to leave his mark on the presidency and on the nation as a whole.

Kennedy presided over a country in the midst of startling social change. In 1960, a new generation was ready to reject the norms and standards of society and venture beyond old taboos and restraints. This generation valued youth, and Kennedy represented a youthful spirit, a stark contrast from that of the elder Eisenhower.

Yet before his third year in office was finished, John Kennedy was felled by an assassin's bullet. The spirit of the 1960s lived on, as would the Kennedy image of youth and vitality, but the nation was forced to mourn the passing of one of its bright young men.

John Fitzgerald Kennedy was born May 29, 1917, in Brookline, Massachusetts. He was born into one of the wealthiest families in America. His father, Joseph Kennedy, was a self-made, Irish millionaire and his mother, Rose Fitzgerald Kennedy, came from a political family. Young John was one of nine children born to the Kennedys. Growing up, John

Kennedy attended a variety of schools including a private academy in Connecticut where he graduated in 1935. He first enrolled at Princeton University and later entered Harvard where he majored in government and international relations. In 1939, he summered in Europe and witnessed firsthand the coming of the events that led to World War II. His European studies led to his senior thesis, which was later published. Titled *Why England Slept*, it became a bestseller.

After America's entry into World War II in December 1941, John Kennedy signed up for duty. He was given command of a PT boat in the Pacific. In August 1943, his boat was attacked by a Japanese cruiser. For his actions, Kennedy was awarded a Purple Heart and the Navy and Marine Corps Medal. Injuries to his back caused Kennedy to leave naval service.

After the war, John's father pushed him into a political career (Joseph had planned to encourage an older brother of JFK's to go into politics, but Joseph, Jr. was killed during the war.) Kennedy ran for the House of Representatives in 1946, and won. Only 29, Kennedy was sometimes mistaken by older congressmen as a congressional pageboy. He was re-elected twice.

In 1952, he ran for the U.S. Senate and won. Just the previous year, JFK had met Jacqueline Lee Bouvier, daughter of a Wall Street broker. They married September 12, 1953. The Kennedys had three children.

Kennedy's political career led him beyond the Congress. In 1956, he campaigned for the Democratic nomination for vice president, but failed. Kennedy then set his sights for the 1960 presidential race.

The Presidency of John F. Kennedy

Having won a seat in the United States Senate in 1958, Kennedy was drawn into the public eye, making him a more legitimate Democratic Party candidate for the 1960 presidential race.

Some Democrats were concerned about a possible Kennedy nomination, citing his religion (he was Roman Catholic and the Democrats had not run a Catholic for president since 1928), and his youth (Kennedy was 43 years old). However, he received his party's nomination for president, and after a close election against Vice President Richard Nixon, Kennedy won by 125,000 votes.

As president, Kennedy pursued an aggressive domestic and foreign agenda. At home, his New Frontier program pushed measures through Congress including an increase in the minimum wage, tariff reductions, economic aid to poor Americans, and a $10 billion tax cut. Although he was slow to move in that direction, he later supported civil rights for America's blacks.

In foreign affairs, Kennedy struggled with major obstacles and challenges, and was not always successful. His plan to liberate Cuba from communist control by supporting a Cuban revolution failed.

The Bay of Pigs invasion was a plan created during the final days of the Eisenhower administration to bring down the communist government of Fidel Castro on the Caribbean island of Cuba. The plan called for the landing of Cuban rebels in Cuba with assistance provided by American forces. When the landing went badly on April 17, 1961, Kennedy withdrew air support from the rebels, and the invasion failed. Kennedy took full responsibility for the invasion and its results.

Despite this earlier failure of Kennedy's foreign policy, he pursued a hard line in dealing with communism. When the Soviet Union attempted to plant nuclear missiles on Cuban soil in 1962, Kennedy faced them down during the Cuban Missile Crisis. He ordered Soviet leadership to remove the missiles or face an American naval blockade of Cuba. The Soviets backed down and removed the missiles.

When the communists raised the Berlin Wall in 1961 to prevent Germans from fleeing East Germany, Kennedy gave his support to the West German people. Kennedy also offered aid to Latin America, saw the formation of the Peace Corps to help Third World peoples, and gave additional support to the South Vietnamese in their struggle against communism.

But Kennedy's time as president was cut short on November 22, 1963. While in Dallas, Texas, he was assassinated by Cuban sympathizer, Lee Harvey Oswald. Oswald had shot the president from a window of the Texas School Book Depository where he worked. Armed with a mail-order rifle, Oswald hit the president from his sixth floor perch as Kennedy's limousine drove past.

The Kennedy assassination is still shrouded in controversy. Questions remain concerning whether Oswald was the only gunman, whether there was a conspiracy, or whether Oswald worked alone. What were Oswald's motivations for killing the president? Such questions may never have definitive answers since Oswald himself was killed two days after the assassination. What remains clear is that America lost one of its leaders through a senseless act of violence.

Review and Write

Do you think Kennedy had greater success in domestic or foreign policy? Explain your answer.

_____

_____

_____

_____

_____

Lyndon B. Johnson

1963–1969

The Rise of Lyndon B. Johnson

Lyndon Baines Johnson was the fourth U.S. vice president to rise to the presidency as a result of assassination. When Lee Harvey Oswald shot President Kennedy in Dallas in November of 1963, Johnson was immediately catapulted to the highest office in the land.

He brought to the White House a wealth of political experience and ability. Johnson is seen as the best example of a forceful American politician. As a leader in the Senate, he was able to get things done and had a reputation as a man who could twist arms to achieve political goals.

Although he became president through assassination in 1963, Johnson went on the next year to be elected in his own right, tallying one of the largest vote margins in American presidential history. He rode this crest of public support into his second term and oversaw one of the most extensive domestic programs—the Great Society.

But that swell of support in 1964 did not last. As Johnson deepened America's military commitment to South Vietnam in its struggle against communism, Johnson's reputation waned. By 1968, the Vietnam War was so unpopular that Johnson's political future was in question. He chose not to run for the presidency a second time. Because of it, in the end, Johnson achieved political praise for his domestic policy, but his venture into Vietnam cost him the presidency.

He was born on August 27, 1908, on the family farm near Stonewall, Texas. Lyndon was the oldest of five children born to Samuel Johnson and Rebekah Baines Johnson. When Lyndon was five, the family moved to Johnson City (named for Lyndon's grandfather). He attended public school and participated in debate.

After high school, he found a job on a road construction crew. In 1927, he enrolled in Southwest Texas State University. He paid for his schooling by working as a janitor. In college, he pursued his interests in debate and politics, graduating in 1930. For a short time, he was a school teacher. In 1931, he was chosen to serve as secretary to a Texas congressman.

In 1934, Lyndon met Claudia Alta Taylor. She had been known as "Lady Bird" since the age of two. After two months of courting, they married in November. The Johnsons had two daughters.

The 1930s marked the rise of Johnson's political star. In 1935, he was appointed by Roosevelt as a state administrator of the National Youth Administration. Two years later, he was elected to the U.S. House. Johnson was re-elected to the House several times and to the Senate in 1948. While in the Senate, Johnson served as the party whip, which made him responsible for making certain his fellow Democrats were present for important votes. He became majority leader in the Senate in 1955. That year, he had his first heart attack. While in the Senate, he championed civil rights laws and the creation of the National Aeronautics and Space Administration (NASA).

The Presidency of Lyndon B. Johnson

In 1960, Johnson announced his interest in being his party's presidential candidate, but he lost that bid to Massachusetts senator, John Kennedy. Johnson gained the vice-presidential nomination, instead. Kennedy and Johnson defeated the Republican challenger, Richard Nixon, in the election. But in 1963, Kennedy's assassination brought Johnson the presidency.

As president, Johnson implemented his social agenda, the Great Society. He called for a tax cut and civil rights laws, as well as a campaign—called the War on Poverty—to provide the poor with jobs and housing. Johnson signed civil rights legislation on July 2, 1964. He sought more funding for education.

But despite Johnson's investment in his War on Poverty, the programs it created failed to significantly alter the level of poverty in America. Most poor people were never helped by Johnson's social programs, and 75 percent of social welfare monies went to the nonpoor.

In 1964, President Johnson ran for re-election. Having completed the term of the late John Kennedy, Johnson had proven himself an effective politician and a man capable of getting things done. He was the obvious pick of the Democratic Party in the summer of 1964. He selected as his vice-presidential running mate, Hubert H. Humphrey, the senator from Minnesota.

The Republicans selected a conservative senator from Arizona, Barry Goldwater. Running with U.S. Representative William E. Miller from New York, Goldwater presented a harsh agenda for Vietnam, hinting he might use nuclear weapons if he considered it necessary. The American people responded overwhelmingly to the Democratic ticket and elected Johnson and Humphrey with 61 percent of the vote.

During Johnson's second administration, America's commitment to South Vietnam was dramatically increased. In 1964, Johnson furthered American involvement in Vietnam (after winning re-election) by calling for ground troops, rather than just advisors. He made the plea for ground troops in August following an alleged incident in the Gulf of Tonkin off the coast of North Vietnam when American naval vessels were fired upon by North Vietnamese gunboats. Congress agreed, passing the Gulf of Tonkin Resolution.

Over the next four years, Johnson increased American troop strength in Vietnam to over half a million. His wartime strategy included the aerial bombing of North Vietnamese targets and arming and training the South with the expectation that the resulting war of "attrition" would diminish the enemy's resolve to fight. It did not.

In 1968, after dropping more than 3 million tons of bombs on Vietnam, the communist opposition was no more prepared to surrender than they had been four years earlier. At home, students protested, calling for demonstrations and riots against the war. The Asian conflict became so unpopular, Johnson announced in March 1968, that he would not seek the party's nomination.

Johnson left the White House in 1969, retired to his ranch in Texas, and wrote his memoirs. After several heart attacks, he died on January 22, 1973.

Review and Write

1. How did Johnson first make his name politically in Texas?

2. How did Johnson's Vietnam policy fail to bring about the results he desired in pursuing war in Southeast Asia?

Richard M. Nixon

1969–1974

The Rise of Richard M. Nixon

The political career of Richard Milhous Nixon was lengthy and complicated. A complex man, Nixon was a staunch anti-communist in his early years. Yet during his presidency, he went to the People's Republic of China—a communist state— and established American diplomatic and cultural ties. He campaigned as a presidential candidate on the issue of law and order, yet he abused political power and violated the Constitution.

The scandal that enveloped his presidency— commonly known as Watergate—brought Nixon's lengthy public service to a disgraceful end. As his involvement in Watergate in 1973 and 1974 became apparent, Nixon was forced to resign the presidency. To date, he stands as the only president to resign from his office.

He was born Richard Milhous Nixon on January 9, 1913, in Yorba Linda, California, just south of Los Angeles. His father was Francis Anthony Nixon and his mother was Hannah Milhous Nixon. Young Richard was raised as a Quaker. He had four brothers.

When he was nine, the family moved to Whittier, California. Richard attended public schools and worked part-time as a handyman, janitor, and as an announcer in an amusement park. He entered the local college, Whittier, which was a Quaker school, at age 17. In 1934, he graduated and then attended Duke University. Nixon received a law degree in 1937.

During the late 1930s, Nixon joined a California law firm and taught a law class at Whittier. He met Thelma Catherine Ryan and they married in 1940. Mrs. Nixon went by the name "Pat," since she was born on St. Patrick's Day. The Nixons had two daughters. Their youngest, Julie, later married the grandson of President Eisenhower.

During World War II, Nixon served in the navy in the Pacific and finished the war with the rank of lieutenant commander. In 1946, back from the war, Nixon entered politics, and was elected to the House and later to the Senate.

While serving in the House, Nixon was a member of the House Un-American Activities Committee (HUAC), which held hearings concerning communist activity in the United States. When a former state department official, Alger Hiss, was accused of being a communist, Nixon pushed for the HUAC to investigate. Hiss was later found guilty in a federal court of perjury when he lied under oath about having passed government secrets to Soviet agents. The Hiss case brought Nixon national attention.

In 1952, the Republican Party turned to Nixon to run as Eisenhower's vice-presidential nominee. He held that post through two terms, serving the country by presiding over cabinet meetings during Eisenhower's absences and traveling to 60 foreign countries.

Nixon prepared to make a run for the presidency in 1960. He gained his party's nomination, yet lost in a close vote count to Democratic challenger John Kennedy. He faced another defeat in 1962 when he failed to win the governorship of California.

The Presidency of Richard Nixon

Despite such political losses, Nixon remained involved in Republican politics.

In 1968, he ran again for the presidency and won over Democratic senator, Hubert Humphrey, of Minnesota. Nixon's presidency promoted a domestic agenda, the New Federalism, which instituted reforms such as revenue sharing between the federal government and the states, and minimum payments to needy families. NASA landed the first men on the moon in 1969, and the courts ordered school desegregation.

Nixon surprised critics during his presidency by supporting new and higher Social Security benefits. He also pushed for increased subsidized housing for the poor. He helped create the Environmental Protection Agency (EPA) and the Occupational Safety and Health Administration (OSHA).

Nixon was a conservative on most civil rights issues. He agreed with school integration in principle, but did not support busing as a means of achieving racial balance.

The nation was paralyzed by the Vietnam War at the time of Nixon's presidency. In March 1969, Nixon ordered a training program for South Vietnamese forces so that they could eventually take over their own fighting and defense (a policy known as *Vietnamization*), and in July he began the gradual withdrawal of U.S. combat troops from Vietnam.

The policy failed however, and, in the spring of 1970, Nixon ordered American ground forces into neighboring Cambodia to rout out enemy hideaways and supply routes. In 1972, Nixon ordered the most extensive bombing of North Vietnamese targets of the entire war.

Such moves brought about renewed war protests on American college campuses. In 1973, Nixon and his foreign policy adviser, Henry Kissinger, negotiated an end to the Vietnam conflict.

In 1972, Nixon faced re-election. He and his vice president were easily accepted by the delegates attending the Republican convention in Miami. The Democrats faced a challenge that year. They nominated a U.S. senator from South Dakota, George S. McGovern, for president. McGovern chose as his running mate, Sargent Shriver, who had directed the Peace Corps during the 1960s and was linked by marriage to the Kennedy family. Nixon was re-elected by a landslide, polling 520 electoral votes and nearly 18 million popular votes. The 1972 election was noted for the fact that it was the first in which 18–year–olds could vote.

Despite Nixon's seeming successes and bold foreign policy, including his ending of the Vietnam War and his support of Israel in 1973 during the Yom Kippur War, his presidency was soon embroiled in a scandal involving a break-in at Democratic headquarters in the Watergate office/apartment complex. When documents and tapes surfaced revealing Nixon's attempt to use the FBI to halt an early investigation of the break-in, Nixon was compelled to resign from the presidency.

Following his resignation, Nixon spent years writing, lecturing, and gaining a reputation as a statesman. He died in 1993.

Review and Write

1. How did Nixon first gain national attention as a politician?

2. Nixon's election in 1968 constituted one of the great returns of an American politician. Explain.

3. Nixon was elected in 1972 by a landslide. But his presidency faced a meltdown over the next two years. What happened?

Gerald Ford

1974–1977

Gerald Ford became president through extra-ordinary circumstances. When Spiro Agnew and Richard Nixon both resigned, Gerald Ford became the first man to become vice president and president of the United States without ever having been elected to either office.

Born July 14, 1913, in Omaha, Nebraska, Ford moved to Grand Rapids, Michigan, with his mother when his parents divorced. When his mother remarried, her new husband adopted Gerald, giving him his last name.

In 1931, Jerry Ford entered the University of Michigan where he played football and succeeded academically. When he graduated in 1935, he was offered contracts with the Green Bay Packers and the Detroit Lions, but turned them both down. He took a coaching job at Yale University instead. In 1938, he entered law school. While a student at Yale, Ford was part owner in a modeling agency and did some modeling of his own. But he later sold his interest in the company. In 1941, he graduated from law school.

During World War II, Ford served in the navy as a physical training director on a Pacific fleet aircraft carrier. After the war, he returned to Michigan and got involved in the local Republican political chapter. In 1947, Gerald Ford met Elizabeth Bloomer, whom he married in 1948. Within days, Ford was elected to the U.S. House of Representatives. (He even campaigned on his wedding day.) The Fords had four children.

While in the House, Ford became the House minority leader in 1965. He sometimes attacked parts of President Johnson's domestic policy. He was an early supporter of Johnson's increasing commitment to the Vietnam War, but in 1967 began seriously speaking out against Johnson's military policies.

In 1972, Ford was elected to his 13th term in the House. The next year, when reports alleged that Vice President Spiro Agnew had taken bribes while Governor of Maryland, Ford's political life changed. After Agnew's resignation, Nixon approached Ford to replace Agnew, with congressional approval. Ford was vice president for less than one year when the Watergate scandal forced Nixon's resignation from office in August 1974.

As president, Ford battled several severe problems —especially a flagging economy. He created public service jobs, and lowered federal income taxes, yet never managed to get an upper hand.

During the spring of 1975, North Vietnamese communist troops defeated South Vietnam, America's former ally. Although Ford asked for aid to South Vietnam, Congress refused. In other foreign policy matters, Ford attempted to follow Nixon's lead by working to better U.S. relations with China and the Soviet Union.

Ford failed to win re-election in 1976. After his presidency, he lectured, wrote his autobiography, and served on corporate boards.

Jimmy Carter

1977–1981

To many, he was an unlikely man to become president of the United States. Jimmy Carter was a soft- spoken, deeply religious man who was not known as a national figure even a year prior to his election to the presidency in 1976. In fact, Carter had never held a national office prior to his presidency. His political experience was limited to the Georgia senate and the governorship.

Yet he defeated the incumbent, President Ford, with the promise that he would never lie to the American people. For a generation disillusioned by Vietnam and Watergate, the promise of honesty and integrity in a presidential candidate appealed to voters, and Carter was given the opportunity to prove himself as a national leader.

James Earl Carter, Jr., was born on October 1, 1924, in the small town that was to be his home all his life—Plains, Georgia. His father was a farmer who also ran a small store. His mother, Lillian Gordy Carter, was a nurse. Carter had three siblings, including one brother.

He attended public school and was known for his good grades and his avid reading. Jimmy graduated from high school in 1941 and entered Georgia Southwestern College. The next year, he received an appointment to the U.S. Naval Academy in Annapolis, Maryland. Jimmy graduated from the academy in 1946, first in his class.

Just prior to his graduation, Carter began dating Rosalynn Smith from Plains. The couple married in the summer of 1946. They had four children. For the next six years, Carter served on battleships and submarines, mostly as an engineering officer. In 1953, when his father died of cancer, Jimmy Carter was compelled to return to his boyhood home and take up the family business. He resigned his commission from the navy.

Once back in Plains, Carter began to run the family peanut farm. The business profited under his direction. He involved himself in local politics and civic organizations. Carter served on the local school board and became a deacon in the Baptist church.

Carter's views on race sometimes failed to win him support among Georgia's white voters. He was opposed to segregation. When his church voted to ban blacks from their membership rolls, Carter's family was one of the few white families to vote against the move.

In the early 1960s, Carter was elected to the Georgia senate. In 1966, he ran as the Democratic candidate for governor, but lost. Four years later, he ran again, and won. As governor, he was known as a political reformer. He was an advocate of black education and increased funding for poor, rural schools. By 1973, he was beginning to eye the presidency of the United States. When he told his mother he was going to run for president, she asked, "President of what?"

The Presidency of Jimmy Carter

Early in 1975, Carter began his campaign for the party's nomination. He was unknown outside his native state of Georgia. He spent approximately 250 days trying to put his name in front of voters that year. But by late fall, polls indicated his chances of becoming president were slim.

Still he went into the Democratic primaries, hopeful. Victories came early that year as Carter won the Iowa caucus in January, followed by success in the New Hampshire primary. Despite challenges from at least ten additional Democratic hopefuls, Carter continued making headway and headlines.

Carter continued to campaign in the spring of 1976 for the Democratic nomination. He campaigned as a Washington outsider and promised the American people he would never lie to them.

Carter emerged from the primaries and the Democratic convention with the nomination, but he faced an incumbent president, Gerald Ford, and his vice-presidential running mate, U.S. Senator Robert J. Dole of Kansas. Confidence in the Republicans was at a low point, clouded by the Watergate scandal and a lackluster economy noted only for its tenacious inflation. The circumstances worked in Carter's favor and he and his running mate, Walter F. Mondale, of Minnesota, went on to defeat President Ford in the election.

As president, Carter created a Department of Energy, pardoned Vietnam-era draft evaders, oversaw a new national energy plan, and battled inflation. But economic problems plagued his administration. By 1980, the inflation rate was 15 percent, an oil shortage was gripping the nation's economy, and Carter found himself facing a 21 percent approval rating.

His foreign policy included successful negotiations between Israel and Egypt in 1978. At the president's invitation, the Israeli prime minister, Menachem Begin, and Egypt's president, Anwar el-Sadat, met at the presidential retreat at Camp David in Maryland. There, President Carter brokered an agreement between the two that helped establish peace between the two powers (the so-called Camp David Accords).

Carter also negotiated a treaty with the Central American nation of Panama to turn the Panama Canal over to the Panamanians by 1999. He worked to develop stronger ties with communist China and sought nuclear arms treaties with the Soviet Union.

But his relations with the Soviet Union were strained during his administration. Carter pushed for human rights recognition in Russia. When the Russians invaded Afghanistan, Carter cut off American wheat exports to the USSR and called for a boycott of the 1980 Olympics held in Moscow. However, when Iranian dissidents took 52 Americans hostage in Tehran, Carter was unable to recover his presidency. His hopes of re-election in 1980 were destroyed by Republican challenger, Ronald Reagan.

Carter retired from politics in 1981 to spend the next 20 years writing, brokering world peace, and performing charity work, such as Habitat for Humanity.

Review and Write

1. What obstacles did Carter have to overcome before he could expect to receive the Democratic Party nomination for president in 1976?

_____

_____

_____

2. What appears to have been the greatest problem the Carter administration faced?

_____

_____

_____

Ronald Reagan

1981–1989

At 69 years of age, former Hollywood actor and governor of California, Ronald Reagan was the oldest president ever elected. (He turned 70 just days after his first inauguration.) Yet Reagan, as president, projected a vigorous image. Perhaps no president of the 20th century, with the possible exception of the Roosevelts, brought more personality to the White House than did Ronald Reagan.

In public, he was a pleasant person, likable, who enjoyed a joke, even at his expense. His motion picture and television background played well to news cameras, and he was able to appeal to the American people with a smile, a wave, and a patriotic salute. Although not a lifelong politician as many previous presidents had been, Reagan was gifted at giving speeches in which he stressed American patriotic values— hard work, self-reliance, patriotic pride, and a strong republic.

He was a conservative Republican who believed the best government was a small one. Reagan's staunch anti-communism defined his presidency, and his foreign policy contributed to the collapse of Eastern European and Soviet communism.

Ronald Reagan was born on February 6, 1911, in Tampico, Illinois. His father, John Edward Reagan, was a shoe salesman, and his mother, Nelle Wilson Reagan, worked part-time as a shop salesclerk.

Growing up, young Ronald was often called "Dutch" by his father. Ronald had one brother named John Neil.

Reagan attended public school in Dixon, Illinois, where he was involved in sports. In the summertime, he worked as a lifeguard. He entered Eureka College in 1928, and paid his own expenses through part-time jobs. At college he became interested in theater. He majored in economics and sociology. Reagan graduated in 1932.

After graduation, he took a job as a sportscaster for an Iowa radio station. Five years later, in 1937, he took a screen test at Warner Brothers and soon received a movie contract. Over the next 20 years, Reagan appeared in over 50 movies. In 1940, he married an actress named Jane Wyman. They had one child and adopted another. After eight years, they divorced.

During World War II, Reagan enlisted but was rejected for combat due to poor eyesight. He spent much of the war making military training films. In 1947, he was elected president of the Screen Actors Guild. In that role, he took part in the anti-communism of the period, and actively sought to eliminate communists from Hollywood.

In 1951, Reagan married another actress, Nancy Davis. This marriage proved enduring and produced two children. From 1954 until 1962, Reagan did television work, hosting dramatic series such as *Death Valley Days,* and *General Electric Theater.*

The Presidency of Ronald Reagan

In 1962, Reagan left the Democratic Party for the Republican. Four years later, he was elected governor of California. He served two terms until 1975. As California's governor, Reagan sent sweeping reform through the state legislature, including cutting the welfare rolls and rerouting state revenues back to local control for local purposes. While governor, he attempted to gain the Republican nomination for president in 1968, but failed. A 1976 challenge of President Gerald Ford also failed.

Four years later, however, following a lackluster term by Democrat Jimmy Carter, the Republican Party chose Reagan as its candidate for president. The 1980 campaign was difficult for Carter. Events in Iran involving over 50 American hostages held by Moslem extremists, and the flagging economy, weakened Carter politically. He hardly campaigned at all, staying close to the White House. Although Reagan avoided discussing the Iranian hostage situation as a courtesy to the president, it was on everyone's mind.

Reagan's win over Carter was extensive. He took over 90 percent of the electoral votes (489 to 49) and garnered 51 percent of the popular vote to Carter's 41 percent. A third party candidate, John B. Anderson, running as an independent, claimed 6.6 percent of the vote. Reagan's win included winning 45 states.

As president, Reagan pursued a conservative agenda, reducing the size of the federal government, supporting tax cuts, and fueling regrowth in the American economy. While Reaganomics jump-started the U.S. economy, it also caused large increases in the national deficit.

His foreign policy included massive increases in military spending—a 35 percent increase during his two terms as president. With his strong, long-standing opposition to communism, Reagan announced plans to deploy missiles to Europe and build a nuclear defense system (known as the Strategic Defense Initiative) involving killer satellites capable of shooting down incoming enemy missiles. He worked to improve relations simultaneously with the Soviet Union.

Reagan also took strong positions against international terrorism. When he learned that Libya financed the bombing of a West Berlin nightspot frequented by American soldiers, Reagan ordered the aerial bombing of the Libyan capital.

Reagan ran for a second term in 1984. His opponent was former Vice President Walter Mondale who chose the first and only female running mate in United States history—U.S. Representative Geraldine Ferraro of New York. Once again, Reagan won the election, this time by an even wider margin of 60 percent. Nearly 25 percent of registered Democrats voted for the Republican president. He even took the majority of the women's vote (54 percent).

His second term was less successful than his first and was marred by foreign policy scandal. In 1986, the story broke of deals made by Reagan officials to sell weapons to Iran (which was illegal) in exchange for the release of American hostages in Lebanon, then using the money to fund anti-communist Contras in Nicaragua. Although congressional hearings were held, Reagan was never directly implicated in the "Iran-Contra" scandal.

Reagan retired after his presidency in 1989, filling his days with speaking engagements and writing. By the mid-1990s, Alzheimer's Disease caused him to withdraw from public life.

Review and Write

Describe Reagan's position on communism.

_____

_____

_____

_____

_____

_____

George Bush

1989–1993

George Bush brought years of public service to the presidency when he was elected in 1988. He had just completed eight years as vice president to President Reagan. Bush had served two terms in the U.S. House of Representatives, was U.S. delegate to the United Nations, special envoy to the People's Republic of China, director of the Central Intelligence Agency, and chairman of the Republican National Committee.

Yet before he became president, he had rarely clearly articulated his political beliefs. After running for the vice president alongside Reagan as a moderate, he turned more conservative during the Reagan presidency. Rarely provided an opportunity to state a clear position of his views for the future of America, he came to the White House with an agenda. He was determined, like Reagan, to promote traditional American values, but by taking a "kinder and gentler" approach.

George Herbert Walker Bush was born in Milton, Massachusetts, on June 12, 1924. His father was Prescott Bush, an investment banker who served in the U.S. Senate. Bush had one sister and three brothers.

As a young man, he attended Phillips Academy in Andover. In 1942, on his 18th birthday, Bush enlisted for service in World War II. He became the youngest navy pilot at the time and flew 58 combat missions in the Pacific. Japanese antiaircraft fire shot Bush down and he had to be rescued by an American submarine. He received the Distinguished Flying Cross.

After the war, Bush married Barbara Pierce. They had six children, one of whom died at age three of leukemia. He later graduated from Yale University with a degree in economics. At Yale, he was a member of Phi Beta Kappa and was an outstanding athlete.

The Bush family then left New England and moved to Texas, where George became involved in the oil industry. He cofounded Zapata Petroleum Corporation in 1953 and remained the company's president until 1964. Politics eventually lured him away from the oil industry.

He ran for the U.S. Senate in 1964 and lost. But two years later, he sought and won a seat in the U.S. House of Representatives. Bush's voting record in the House revealed a man who was both conservative and moderate. He tended to support President Nixon's policies regarding the Vietnam War.

In 1970, Bush ran for the Senate once again and lost. President Nixon, however, would soon appoint Bush as Permanent Representative of the U.S. to the United Nations. In 1973, Nixon supported Bush as chairman of the Republican National Committee. Despite earlier support from Nixon, Bush suggested that Nixon resign the presidency in August of 1974 at the height of the Watergate scandal.

From 1974 to 1975, President Ford asked Bush to serve as liaison to the People's Republic of China.

At the end of 1975, Ford appointed Bush as director of the CIA, the federal government's spy agency. Two years later, Bush left public service and chaired the board of the First National Bank of Houston.

The Presidency of George Bush

In 1980, Bush entered the Republican race for the presidential nomination. He lost to Reagan but was chosen as his running mate. During the Reagan presidency, Bush visited dozens of countries and worked on antidrug programs at home.

In 1988, he ran for the presidency against Democratic challenger, Michael Dukakis, of Massachusetts. The Democratic Party felt it had a reasonable opportunity that year to regain the White House from the Republicans. In early polls, Dukakis appeared ahead of Bush. But Bush's strategists painted the liberal Massachusetts governor as a man who had opposed the death penalty and mandatory school prayer and had vetoed a law that required students to pledge allegiance to the American flag. As the election approached in November, Bush pulled ahead of his opponent and won the popular vote by a margin of 54 to 46 percent and carried 40 of the 50 states electorally. Bush and his running mate, Dan Quayle, of Indiana, found themselves in power in Washington.

As president, Bush was more moderate than Reagan. He promised not to raise taxes, a promise he did not keep in the end. He did sign a bill increasing new jobs through increased exports.

During the Bush presidency, communism collapsed in Eastern Europe and the Soviet Union, the Berlin Wall was dismantled, and East and West Germany were reunited for the first time since World War II.

But President Bush will be best remembered for his pursuit of the Persian Gulf War from 1990 to 1991 against Saddam Hussein of Iraq. On August 2, 1990, Iraqi troops invaded neighboring Kuwait. The invasion was swift and successful, backed by 850 Iraqi tanks. President Bush responded almost immediately, calling for the deployment of American forces to the Middle East to be stationed in Saudi Arabia. This action was called "Operation Desert Shield."

With the independence of Kuwait at stake, as well as the security of Kuwaiti oil reserves, Bush organized a coalition of nations against Iraq. He appealed through the United Nations for an armed response. Two months after the Iraqi invasion, the U.S. had 230,000 troops in the Persian Gulf region.

In November, President Bush changed American military policy in the Gulf from one of defense to offense. He increased U.S. forces (whose number was augmented by forces from other countries) to 580,000 by January 1991. His "Desert Shield" became "Desert Storm," which resulted in 42 days of bombing and troop movements against the Iraqis by American and Allied forces. By the last week of February, Saddam's forces had been pushed out of Kuwait, and 100,000 Iraqi soldiers had been killed. Bush's popularity among Americans soared after the war.

Yet, despite his popularity, he faced a serious challenge for re-election in 1992. A national recession was the chief issue of that campaign. Critics of both Bush and Reagan pointed to a national debt of $4 trillion. Bush's opponents during the election were Democratic challenger, Bill Clinton, of Arkansas, and H. Ross Perot, of Texas, who ran as the Reform Party candidate. Clinton won the election with 43 percent of the vote to Bush's 38 percent.

Following his presidency, Bush spent time with his family and made public appearances. In 2000, he worked on behalf of son George W. Bush's campaign for president.

Review and Write

Describe how Bush organized military efforts against Saddam Hussein following Iraq's invasion of Kuwait in 1990.

_____

_____

_____

_____

Bill Clinton

1993–2001

The last president of the 20th century, Bill Clinton was the fifth chief executive of the century to serve two complete terms. Elected in 1992 at the age of 46, Clinton was one of our youngest presidents. His youth and vitality played well with the voters, and he used his terms to reform social policy.

Yet the Clinton presidency was plagued from the outset with bitter partisan politics. In addition, some of his social positions—especially the issue of national health insurance—created a firestorm of controversy and bitter political fights. Complicating matters, Clinton became embroiled in a scandal involving personal misconduct.

He was born William Jefferson Blythe IV, on August 19, 1946, in the small town of Hope, Arkansas. His father was killed in an auto accident three months before William's birth. His mother then married Roger Clinton who adopted young William.

Bill Clinton proved an excellent student, growing up in Hot Springs. At age 16, he was selected as a delegate to the American Legion Boy's Nation Program and attended a convention in Washington, D.C. There, young Bill met President Kennedy who would prove to be Clinton's inspiration to pursue a political career.

Clinton went to college at Georgetown University where he received his undergraduate degree in international affairs in 1968. Chosen as a Rhodes scholar, he studied at Oxford University for two years, then received a law degree from Yale University in 1973.

With his academic career under way, Clinton returned to Arkansas where he taught law at the University of Arkansas. His political career kicked off early with his election as attorney general of Arkansas in 1976. Bill Clinton had earlier married a Wellesley College graduate, Hillary Rodham, whom he had met while studying law at Yale. The Clintons had only one daughter, Chelsea, who was born in 1980.

In 1978, he was elected governor of Arkansas. Four years later, he lost a re-election bid. Clinton ran for re-election as attorney general in 1980 and lost, having angered the voters by raising automobile licensing fees. But he came back in 1982, and proceeded to win five consecutive terms as Arkansas governor, bringing him to the year 1992.

That year, Clinton ran as the Democratic nominee for president. He chose Al Gore from Tennessee as his running mate. With Gore, age 44, and Clinton, age 46, the ticket had a youthful appeal to voters. Clinton defeated President Bush and third-party candidate, Ross Perot.

Economic issues had worked to defeat Bush, and the new president set to work to revitalize the economy. He supported budget deficit reductions and eventually balanced the federal budget. In his later years as president, the country even experienced budget surpluses.

The Presidency of Bill Clinton

Significant trade agreements with Mexico and Canada—the North American Free Trade Agreement—became a reality. NAFTA made the importation and exportation of goods and services, and international investments between the United States and Canada easier by abolishing all tariff restrictions and other barriers to trade. The spirit and intent of the treaty was to create a massive free trade zone involving a total trade population of 360 million people experiencing a $6 trillion, three-nation economy.

By 1994, Clinton's efforts in trade legislation led to another significant treaty called GATT—General Agreement on Tariffs and Trade. While this agreement between the United States and other nations did not immediately eliminate all tariffs between member nations, it slashed tariffs on many imports, eliminated import quotas, and established the World Trade Organization to settle trade disputes between countries.

Other Clinton programs went into effect, as well. Welfare reform as enacted by Congress, and the Family and Medical Leave Act became law, protecting the jobs of parents who care for their sick children.

The campaign launched by Clinton and First Lady Hillary Rodham to create national health insurance met with stiff resistance and failed. Yet health insurance coverage for millions of uninsured Americans continued to be a priority for Clinton. Throughout his years in the White House, he was able to expand insurance for children through Medicaid, as well as through the state Children's Health Insurance program (CHIP). By the final year of his presidency, his administration was pushing for a $110 billion health care initiative designed to provide medical coverage to 5 million uninsured Americans.

During his presidency, Clinton appointed two new members to the Supreme Court.

In foreign policy, the president committed troops to trouble spots, such as Haiti, Somalia, and Kosovo in the Balkans. In 1994, he sent troops to Kuwait, and in 1996 ordered air strikes against Iraq.

In 1996, Clinton faced re-election. Already his presidency was under investigation for various scandals. Questions regarding his sexual activities while governor of Arkansas dominated the news, and Clinton was already the target of a sexual harassment civil suit filed by a former Arkansas government employee. Such scandals dominated the rhetoric of U.S. Senator Robert Dole of Kansas—the Republican Party's presidential nominee in the 1996 election. Dole struggled to overcome the popularity of the Clinton administration and eventually lost the election.

After his re-election in 1996, Clinton faced a serious challenge in the form of a political and personal scandal involving his alleged sexual activity with a White House intern. When Clinton was revealed as having lied about his involvement, impeachment proceedings ensued, but attempts to remove him from office failed. Despite such challenges, Clinton's approval rating among the American people remained high into the final year of his presidency.

Review and Write

1. Describe the successes and failures of Clinton's involvement in Arkansas politics.

_____

_____

_____

2. What strides did Clinton make in providing government-financed medical coverage for America's uninsured? What failures did he face in this area?

_____

_____

_____

_____

George W. Bush

2001–

George W. Bush was born July 6th, 1946, and grew up in Midland and Houston, Texas. His parents are former vice president and president of the United States George Herbert Walker Bush and Barbara Bush. George W. received a bachelor's degree from Yale University and an MBA from Harvard Business School. He served as an F-102 pilot for the Texas Air National Guard.

In 1977, Bush met and married Laura Welch, a librarian. (The couple had two children— twin girls, Jenna and Barbara, named for their grandmothers.) The same year George took $17,000 from his education trust fund to set up an oil company called Arbusto Energy (*arbusto* means "Bush" in Spanish), which failed when oil prices fell. Despite several attempts to revive the business (first by changing the company's name and later merging with other companies), it didn't succeed. In 1990, Bush sold his remaining stock and left the oil business.

Bush spent 1986 and 1987 working on his father's presidential campaign as adviser and speech-writer. (He moved to Washington in 1987 to devote full-time to the campaign.) After the election he returned to Texas, and assembled a group of investors to buy the Texas Rangers baseball team for $86 million. Although Bush only invested $606,000, he was named managing partner—a position he held until his election as governor of Texas.

Bush moved back to Washington in 1991 to work as an adviser on his father's re-election campaign. Then in 1993, Bush announced his plans to run for governor of Texas. He won the 1994 gubernatorial election with 53.5 percent of the vote.

Over the next four years, Bush was a popular Republican governor. In 1998, he ran for re-election and became the first Texas governor to be elected to consecutive four-year terms. Bush's margin of victory was even greater in the '98 election, as he garnered nearly 70 percent of the vote, including half the Hispanic vote, 27 percent of the African-American vote, and 65 percent of the women's vote. One out of every four Democratic voters cast ballots for George W. in that election.

In 1999, the Bushes decided that George should run for president of the United States. During the spring of 2000, he campaigned for the Republican nomination, receiving serious challenge from Arizona senator John McCain. Vice President Al Gore ran against former New Jersey senator Bill Bradley for the Democratic nomination.

After Bush and Gore became official candidates in the summer of 2000, they led spirited campaigns. Bush selected Dick Cheney—former secretary of defense during his father's presidency—as his vice-presidential running mate, while Gore named Joe Lieberman—U.S. senator from Connecticut and the first Jewish-American to run for the vice-presidency.

On November 7, 2000, the closest election in

United States history began with a night of errors for the major television networks. Pundits first declared the state of Florida for Gore—making an electoral victory by Bush unlikely. As the night went on, newscasters retracted their call, but made it clear that Florida voters would determine the election. A little after 2 a.m. eastern time the networks made another premature call, declaring Florida for Bush, setting in motion a concession call by Gore. As Gore was about to make his concession speech, word reached him that Florida was "too close to call." Gore called Bush and recanted his concession. Most Americans went to sleep that night believing Bush had won the election,but woke to learn that neither candidate had received enough electoral votes (a required minimum of 270) to be declared president.

Voter confusion, and inconsistencies in ballot counting (along with a sizeable number of absentee ballots from overseas voters) in the state of Florida became the focal point of the heated post-election controversy. More than 19,000 votes were disqualified in West Palm Beach, Florida due to problems—especially among elderly voters—with the confusing design of the so-called "butterfly ballot." Voters in that heavily Democratic county claimed to have accidentally voted for Reform Party candidate Pat Buchanan instead of Al Gore.

In addition, several thousand ballots were mechanically rejected when voting machines could not detect punched votes on ballot cards raising questions as to the reliability of machine counting.

Given the closeness of the vote and multiple irregularities in the election process, the Gore campaign demanded a manual recount of the ballots in four crucial Florida counties. (A machine recount had given Bush a lead of 288 votes.)

Court cases were filed on both sides as state deadlines for the vote's final report loomed and voting officials painstakingly hand counted ballots. State officials were asked to interpret voter intent based on the appearance of the ballots' chad—the small rectangular pieces which are punched through and removed when a voter makes his or her selection. Initially, counters were told to count only "hanging chad"—holes clearly punched through with chad hanging by one or two corners—

but the election board later ruled—after pressure from the Democratic Party—that counters could accept chad with apparent indentation (a "dimpled chad") that had not been pushed through.

Cases appeared before Florida County Circuit Judges, the Florida Supreme Court, and finally the United States Supreme Court. On December 11, Supreme Court justices heard oral arguments from lawyers representing both candidates regarding whether the Florida Supreme Court had rewritten state election law upon ordering a manual statewide recount of ballots discarded by the vote counting machines. The next day, the federal justices overturned the ruling of the state court by a vote of 5 to 4, and ruled that no further recounts could take place. Florida Secretary of State Katherine Harris—a Republican—certified the election and granted Florida's 25 electoral votes to Bush.

With this decision, Vice President Al Gore appeared on national television and conceded victory to his opponent. It was the closest election in American history, and the first to be determined by a court decision. Although Gore won the popular vote by over 500,000 votes, Bush's electoral victory (271 to 267—a slim 4-vote margin) won him the election. Bush was the first popular-vote loser to claim the White House since 1888. Many analysts expect a reexamination of the electoral college as well as ballot reform and review of the national voting process as an outcome of this historic election.

Review and Write

Discuss whether the electoral college continues to serve the democratic process or whether it is—as some analysts have said—a political dinosaur.

Test IV

Part I.

Multiple Choice.

Match the information at the left to the answers on the right. Place the letter of the correct answer in the spaces below.

1. He provided supplies to West Berlin through the Berlin airlift.
2. The Bay of Pigs invasion of Cuba took place during his presidency.
3. His War on Poverty provided the poor with jobs and housing.
4. This future president provided the plans for the D-Day Invasion.
5. He contracted polio as a young adult.
6. He worked as a Texas school teacher.
7. He was raised in the Church of the Brethren in Christ, a pacifist group.
8. The Civil Conservation Corps was created during his presidency.
9. The Gulf of Tonkin Resolution was passed during his presidency.
10. This future president commanded a PT boat during World War II.
11. His Marshall Plan helped rebuild Europe after World War II.
12. He held the position of assistant secretary of the navy.

A. John F. Kennedy
B. Franklin D. Roosevelt
C. Dwight D. Eisenhower
D. Harry S. Truman
E. Lyndon B. Johnson

Answers:

1. ____ 2. ____ 3. ____ 4. ____ 5. ____ 6. ____ 7. ____ 8. ____ 9. ____ 10. ____ 11. ____ 12. ____

Part II.

Multiple Choice.

Match the information at the left to the answers on the right. Place the letter of the correct answer in the spaces below.

1. He coached football at Yale University.
2. Growing up, he was known by the nickname "Dutch."
3. He and Henry Kissinger negotiated an end to the Vietnam War.
4. He served as governor of California before his presidency.
5. He ran a peanut farm in Georgia.
6. As a younger man, he was co-owner of a modeling agency.
7. During World War II, he flew combat missions in the Pacific.
8. He served on the House Un-American Activities Committee.
9. American hostages were held in Iran during his presidency.
10. He became embroiled in a sex scandal during his second term.
11. He was not elected vice president or president, but served as both.
12. He was raised in the Quaker faith.

A. Richard Nixon
B. Ronald Reagan
C. Jimmy Carter
D. Bill Clinton
E. George H. W. Bush
F. Gerald R. Ford

Answers:

1. ____ 2. ____ 3. ____ 4. ____ 5. ____ 6. ____ 7. ____ 8. ____ 9. ____ 10. ____ 11. ____ 12. ____

Answers

Page 3

1. Answers will vary, but should include serving as commander in chief of the armed forces, making treaties, appointing ambassadors and Supreme Court justices, enforcing the laws of the land and receiving foreign ambassadors and ministers. Other possible answers could include pardoning citizens and postponing punishments for criminals.

2. Answers will vary, but typical answers will include such presidents as Washington, Lincoln, Jefferson, the Roosevelts, Kennedy, Reagan, etc.

Page 5

1. Washington led the Continental army through the American Revolution, served as the first U.S. president, and was an American patriot.

2. His great-grandfather settled in America. He was a sailor whose ship ran aground in the Potomac River in 1656 or 1657. While waiting for the ship to be repaired, he decided to remain in Virginia.

3. He weighed 175 pounds, had a large and straight nose, blue-gray penetrating eyes, and dark brown hair. He stood over 6 feet, two inches in height, was broad-shouldered, and well-built.

Page 7

1. The French blamed him for killing a French ambassador, thereby leading to a conflict that turned into the French and Indian War.

2. He married and expanded his estate at Mt. Vernon. He became involved in the revolutionary politics of the day and opposed England's policies of taxation on the colonies.

Page 9

1. He led the Continental army through the war from 1775 until its conclusion in 1783. Washington's greatness was in his ability to maintain an army in the field against a superior force.

2. Crises were: war between England and France and the pressure to take sides; domestic rebellion in Pennsylvania over whiskey taxes; a poor economy; and challenges from Britain and Spain.

Page 11

1. Adams spoke out against British taxes by writing pamphlets. He defended the British soldiers responsible for the Boston Massacre. He supported Washington for commander of continental forces.

2. He served in the Continental Congresses helping to draft the Declaration of Independence; was a diplomat to France; and negotiated the peace treaty ending the Revolutionary War.

3. Challenges were a naval war with France and Britain; France refusing to negotiate without first receiving bribes.

Page 15

1. Jefferson's talents included his skills as a political theorist, writer, philosopher, diplomat, and educator.

2. He wrote pamphlets, organized nonimportation agreements, served in the Continental Congress, drafted the Declaration of Independence, and served as governor of Virginia.

3. Jefferson wrote the Declaration of Independence, and wrote of equality but owned slaves. Even when he became convinced that slavery was evil, he continued to own slaves until his death in 1826.

Page 17

1. Madison proposed the checks and balances system for the federal government which developed into the federal government with its three branches: legislative, judicial, and executive. Madison attended the Constitutional Convention having read dozens of books in preparation, and he took the most detailed notes of the Convention.

2. It gave Americans a new sense of nationalism. It no longer had to worry about threats from Great Britain.

Page 19

1. Monroe was not a quick thinker or fiery speaker or skilled writer. He thought honestly and thoughtfully. He pursued his goals with personal warmth and found he could turn the minds of those around him with the power of his charm and character.

2. He helped negotiate the Louisiana Purchase and the annexation of Florida from the Spanish.

3. His foreign policies produced viable treaties with Great Britain and Spain. He issued his Monroe Doctrine to extend American influence to the nations of Latin America.

Page 21

1. Both Adamses served a single term as president. They were highly intellectual and well educated. They had trouble in social encounters with anyone other than close friends. They felt strongly about the U.S. and the republic's future.

2. Although he was officially a Federalist, he often voted alongside the Democratic-Republicans. He also stood up against the political positions of Andrew Jackson, who was very popular with the people.

3. Adams was not a southerner nor did he own slaves.

Page 25

1. Jackson's exploits were extremely important in establishing him as a national figure, something that

had to occur before he could rise in the political arena of national government. His military exploits, especially the Battle of New Orleans (1815) catapulted him to the public scene and made his name a household word. Such public activities also helped people identify with him as a frontiersman, Indian fighter, general, and Westerner.

Page 26: Test I

Part I.
1. C 2. B 3. A 4. A 5. B 6. B 7. A 8. H 9. H 10. E 11. A 12. A

Part II.
1. D 2. A 3. C 4. A 5. D 6. A 7. A 8. B 9. B 10. A 11. A 12. C

Page 28

1. Van Buren believed in a prosperous and growing America, while advocating the belief that "the less government interferes, the better for general prosperity."

2. His political philosophy caused him to do little to battle the depression.

3. He served as Jackson's secretary of state and he improved U.S. and British relations. He also served as Jackson's second vice president. He constantly offered his support to Jackson and his policies.

Page 29

Answers will vary, but Harrison's military career put him in the public eye more than did his political successes. As a general and territorial governor, he fought Indians and this made him a popular figure in America in that time period.

Page 30

The Whigs nominated Tyler for the vice-presidency on the belief that he supported the restoration of the Bank of the U.S. and that he supported higher tariffs. When he became president upon Harrison's death, he surprised the Whigs by vetoing their attempts to do both.

Page 32

1. Polk ran for the presidency in 1844 and campaigned on the promises of annexing western territory such as the Oregon Country and Texas.

2. He attempted to buy California, and when he failed, he goaded the Mexicans into a war.

3. Answers will vary. Whether one agrees with Polk's political goals, he did achieve success during his presidency because he accomplished everything he promised the American people, including the annexation of Texas and Oregon.

Page 33

Military heroes such as Zachary Taylor were popular with the American people. They admired such people and felt compelled to reward them with political office.

Page 34

Although Fillmore was opposed to slavery personally, he supported the Compromise of 1850 because he wanted to hold the Union together. Such a position on his part helped to postpone the Civil War by perhaps a decade.

Page 36

1. Pierce had supported the Kansas-Nebraska Act, which had opened up the territory to possible slavery. Pierce found himself unable to adequately deal with the violence taking place in "Bleeding Kansas."

2. His wife was ill with tuberculosis and prone to depression. Two of her children had died young, which saddened her deeply. She did not enjoy political occasions. She convinced Pierce to abandon his earlier political career. After his election, Pierce and his wife witnessed the death of their 11-year-old son in a railroad accident.

Page 38

1. Buchanan served in the Pennsylvania assembly; was elected to the U.S. House of Representatives in 1820; was appointed minister to Russia; served as a U.S. Senator; was appointed as secretary of state; negotiated for the Mexican cession after the Mexican War; and served as minister to Great Britain.

2. National conflict over the issue of the expansion of slavery. Problems in Kansas over slavery came to a head during his presidency.

Page 42

1. Young Lincoln's pioneer experiences included living in a lean-to log cabin, learning to wield an ax, doing farm chores, and receiving little formal education.

2. **Successes:** Ran for state legislature in 1834 and won, serving four terms. Ran for the U.S. House of Representatives as a Whig and again won. Became a well-known lawyer and had a successful practice.

   Failures: Ran for the U.S. Senate in 1858 against Stephen Douglas and lost.

Page 43

1. Answers will vary. Students will consider it difficult for someone of humble origins to become president because elections require millions of dollars.

2. Answers will vary. The Republicans have a clear agenda in 1867 when they pass the Tenure of Office Act through Congress. They want Johnson to challenge the law and Congressional authority. By doing so, radical Republicans could pursue an impeachment of the president. Students should have questions about how the Republican congressional leadership is behaving on this one.

Page 46

1. Grant did not enjoy his stations of duty during his early military experience. He began drinking while separated from his wife and family. He failed at farming and various other jobs.

2. As with earlier presidents—Washington, Jackson, Taylor, for example—a man's military career could provide a stepping stone to a political career including the presidency. Grant became famous nationally through his generalship during the Civil War. Without this reputation, he probably would not have run for the presidency, much less win it.

Page 27: Test II

Part I.
    1. C 2. A 3. G 4. F 5. C 6. E 7. A 8. F 9. D 10. A 11. B 12. E

Part II.
    1. C 2. A 3. D 4. B 5. C 6. B 7. A 8. D 9. A 10. A 11. D 12. A

Page 49

1. Hayes was actively involved in the Underground Railroad prior to the Civil War, helping slaves escape. He campaigned for voting rights for blacks.

2. Hayes appears to have been a good president. He ended Reconstruction which was bitterly hated by many Southerners. He instituted civil service reform in the federal government. He appointed cabinet members on the basis of their merits. He pursued a conservative monetary policy.

Page 50

1. Garfield was shot by a deranged man who had sought a public office from President Garfield and had been turned down. He felt he had helped elect Garfield by writing a political pamphlet, but in fact the pamphlet was never distributed. The assassin felt that Garfield owed him political favors, and when Garfield didn't prove responsive, Charles Guiteau shot the president.

Page 51

Arthur began implementing civil service reform after he became president. He backed the passage of the Pendleton Civil Service Act.

Page 53

1. Cleveland attempted to clean up the corrupt city government of Buffalo. He was an honest governor. As president, he instructed his officials to cut waste and corruption in their departments. He pursued dis-honest railroad companies and opposed handing out pensions to veterans with questionable claims. He pursued a sound monetary policy. He refused to pursue annexation of Hawaii because he felt Americans had been too involved. He helped settle a boundary dispute between England and Venezuela.

Page 55

1. Harrison's great-grandfather signed the Declaration of Independence. His grandfather was a former president, and his father had served in the U.S. Congress.

2. Farmers abandoned the Republicans and supported the Populist Party. Factory workers also voted Populist, since Harrison's administration had responded negatively to labor unrest during his term.

Page 57

1. The Mckinley's were very close. He was known for his kindness to her. He took care of her during her illnesses, including epilepsy.

2. The United States gained control of Cuba, the Philippines, Puerto Rico, Hawaii, American Samoa, and Guam during McKinley's administration. The United States fought and won a war with the Spanish to free Cuba.

Page 60

1. Within his first year as president, Roosevelt began a policy of reining in the excesses of the big trusts. His Justice Department filed suit against such trusts. In all, 43 suits were filed by the Roosevelt administration.

2. Answers will vary, but could include: his trust-busting activities, support of struggling labor unions, his conservation efforts, his push for governmental inspection of meatpacking plants and for pure food and drugs, his support of the Monroe Doctrine, his mediation of the Russo-Japanese War.

Page 62

Taft was much less drawn to the public eye. He was quieter and less dramatic and showy. He did not enjoy his presidency nor did he aspire to become president as Roosevelt did.

Page 65

1. Wilson was known as an academic, scholar, writer, university football coach, publisher of textbooks, president of Princeton University, and progressive governor of New Jersey.

Page 67

1. Answers will vary, but Harding's most obvious error could have been his failure to pick honest men for his cabinet. Such men fell into corruption during the Harding presidency.

Page 69

1. Coolidge did not recognize the right of policemen to strike.

2. He worked to reduce the national debt by $1 billion. He called for the reduction of the income tax. The Coolidge years were prosperous. His secretary of state negotiated treaties to end war.

Page 71

1. In 1908, Hoover formed his own mining engineering company. His pursuit of a career as a mining engineer ultimately made him a millionaire.

2. When he happened to find himself in London in the summer of 1914, he was asked by U.S. government officials to organize a food relief program for starving Belgians. When he returned to the U.S., President Wilson put him in charge of the U.S. Food Administration. Such work made him internationally known.

Page 72: Test III

Part I.
   1. F   2. B   3. G   4. A   5. C   6. E   7. G   8. F   9. D   10. C   11. A   12. B

Part II.
   1. E   2. B   3. D   4. C   5. B   6. D   7. A   8. E   9. B   10. E   11. A   12. C

Page 75

1. Roosevelt was elected to the New York senate, served as assistant secretary of the navy, and was elected governor of New York state.

2. The Hundred Days refers to the first three months of FDR's first administration as president. They were the significant early days of the sweeping legislation of the New Deal that FDR introduced to battle the Great Depression.

3. These were the years of direct American involvement in World War II. Such involvement in war is difficult on a president. FDR had to set strategy and participate in international conferences, which were taxing on him.

Page 77

Truman did not trust Stalin and often took a hard stance against the Soviets. He stood firm against communism and its aggression around the world in places such as Greece, Turkey, Eastern Europe, and

Korea. When the Soviets blocked Western access to West Berlin, Truman ordered an airlift of food, supplies, and medicines. He supported the Nationalist Chinese against communist forces. He aided South Korea against communist North Korean aggression backed by the Soviet Union.

Page 79

Answers will vary. Eisenhower was successful both as a military leader and as president of the United States. Probably he enjoyed his role as military leader more than he did his presidency.

Page 81

Answers will vary. Kennedy's domestic policy successes included an increase in the minimum wage, tariff reductions, economic aid to poor Americans, and a $10 billion tax cut. He supported civil rights for America's blacks. His foreign policy successes included forcing the removal of Soviet missiles from Cuba, support to the West German people following the erection of the Berlin Wall, aid to Latin America, the formation of the Peace Corps, and additional support to the South Vietnamese in their struggle against communism.

Page 83

1. In 1935, Johnson was appointed by FDR as a state administrator of the National Youth Administration. He was elected to the U.S. House and later to the Senate. In the Senate, he served as the party whip, and he became majority leader in the Senate in 1955.

2. Johnson always believed that if he invested enough men and material in South Vietnam, that he would be able to turn the tide against the communists. He called for the aerial bombing of North Vietnam. But his war of attrition did not kill the enemy's resolve to fight.

Page 85

1. While serving in the U.S. House, Nixon was a member of the House Un-American Activities Committee, which held hearings concerning communist activity in the United States. When a former state department official, Alger Hiss, was accused of being a communist, Nixon pushed for the HUAC to investigate. His was later found guilty. The Hiss case brought Nixon national attention.

2. While serving as vice president for Eisenhower, Nixon ran for the presidency in 1960. He lost that election, went into private law practice and then ran for the governorship of California in 1962. Again, he was defeated. Yet Nixon's political career was not over. He ran for the presidency in 1968 and won.

3. Nixon's presidency became embroiled in scandal in 1973 involving a break-in at Democratic campaign headquarters in the Watergate office/apartment complex. When documents and tapes surfaced revealing Nixon's attempt to use the FBI to halt an early investigation of the break-in, Nixon was compelled to resign from the presidency.

Page 88

1. Carter was a relative unknown as late as 1975. He spent 250 days trying to put his name in front of

voters that year, and eventually his hard work paid off when he received his party's nomination.

2. Carter faced at least two overarching problems during his presidency and both answers by students should be acceptable. The economy during the Carter administration was extremely poor. The inflation rate was 15 percent and an oil shortage was gripping the nation. The other problem was the Iranian hostage crisis. For 444 days—the last year of Carter's presidency—the Iranians held 52 Americans hostage in Tehran. Carter was unable to negotiate or force their release.

Page 90

Reagan was adamantly opposed to communism during his entire political life. As president of the Screen Actors Guild in 1947, he took an active part in fighting communism and sought to eliminate communists from Hollywood. As a U.S. president, Reagan built up the American arsenal against the Soviet Union. His administration covertly supplied weapons to the Nicaraguan Contras in their struggle against communist rule.

Page 92

After Iraq invaded neighboring Arab nation, Kuwait, Bush organized an international response. He called for deployment of American forces to the Middle East and organized a coalition of nations against Iraq. By early 1991, Bush launched Desert Storm against the Iraqis and pushed them out of Kuwait.

Page 94

1. Clinton won election as Arkansas governor in 1978 and four years later was defeated for re-election. In 1980 he ran for re-election as attorney general of Arkansas and lost. In 1982, he won the first of five consecutive terms as Arkansas governor.

2. He expanded insurance for children through Medicaid, as well as through the state Children's Health Insurance Program (CHIP). He also supported the Family and Medical Leave Act, which became law during his administration. The law protected the jobs of parents who care for their sick children.

Page 96

Answers will vary.

Page 97: Test IV

Part I.
   1. D   **2.** A   **3.** E   **4.** C   **5.** B   **6.** E   **7.** C   **8.** B   **9.** E   **10.** A   **11.** D   **12.** B

Part II.
   1. F   **2.** B   **3.** A   **4.** B   **5.** C   **6.** F   **7.** E   **8.** A   **9.** C   **10.** D   **11.** F   **12.** A

Bibliography

INTRODUCTION

Will Cleveland, *Yo, Millard Fillmore!: And All Those Presidents You Don't Know* (Brookfield, CT: Millbrook Press, 1997).

William A. DeGregorio and Connie Jo Dickerson, *The Complete Book of U.S. Presidents: From George Washington to Bill Clinton* (New York: Random House, 1997).

Victoria Sherrow, *The Big Book of U.S. Presidents* (Philadelphia: Running Press Book Publishers, 1994).

George A Sullivan. *Mr. President: A Book of U.S. Presidents* (New York: Scholastic, Inc., 1996).

GEORGE WASHINGTON

Richard Brookhiser, *Founding Father: Rediscovering George Washington* (New York: The Free Press, 1997).

John E. Ferling. *Setting the World Ablaze: Washington, Adams, Jefferson and the American Revolution* (New York: Oxford University Press, Incorporated, 2000).

William Martin, *Citizen Washington* (New York: Warner Books, Incorporated. Mass Market Paperback, 1999).

Willard Sterne Randall, *George Washington* (New York: Henry Holt & Company, 1984).

Augusta Stevenson, *George Washington: Young Leader* (Childhood of Famous Americans Series) (New York: Macmillan Publishing Company, Incorporated, 1984).

JOHN ADAMS

John Murray Allison, *Adams and Jefferson: The Story of a Friendship* (Norman: University of Oklahoma Press, 1966).

Catherine Drinker Bowen, *John Adams and the American Revolution* (Boston: Little, Brown, 1950).

Ralph Brown, *The Presidency of John Adams* (Lawrence: University Press of Kansas, 1975).

John E. Ferling, *John Adams: A Life* (New York: Henry Holt & Company, Incorporated, 1999).

Page Smith, *John Adams* (Garden City, N.Y.: Doubleday, 1962).

THOMAS JEFFERSON

A&E Biography Video: *Thomas Jefferson: Philosopher of Freedom*.

Stephen Ambrose, *Undaunted Courage: Meriwether Lewis, Thomas Jefferson, and the Opening of the American West* (New York: Simon & Schuster, 1997).

Fawn Brodie, *Thomas Jefferson, An Intimate History* (New York: Norton, 1974).

Joseph J. Ellis, *American Sphinx: The Character of Thomas Jefferson* (New York: Random House, 1998).

Roger G. Kennedy, *Burr, Hamilton, and Jefferson: A Study in Character* (New York: Oxford University Press, Incorporated, 2000).

Helen Albee Monsell, *Thomas Jefferson: Third President of the United States (Childhood of Famous Americans Series)* (New York: Simon & Schuster, 1989).

Garry Wills, *Thomas Jefferson: Genius of Liberty* (New York: Studio Books, 2000).

JAMES MADISON

Jean Fritz, *The Great Little Madison* (New York: Putnam, 1989).

Ralph Louis Ketcham, *James Madison: A Biography* (Charlottesville: University Press of Virginia, 1990).

Drew R. McCoy, *The Last of the Fathers: James Madison and the Republican Legacy* (Cambridge, UK: Cambridge University Press, 1991).

JAMES MONROE

Harry Ammon, *James Monroe: The Quest for National Identity* (Charlottesville: University Press of Virginia, 1990).

Noble Cunningham, *The Presidency of James Monroe* (Lawrence: University Press of Kansas, 1996).

Wendie C. Old, *James Monroe* (Springfield, NJ: Enslow Publishers, Incorporated, 1998).

JOHN QUINCY ADAMS

Lynn Parsons, *John Quincy Adams* (Madison, Wisconsin: Madison House, 1998).

ANDREW JACKSON

Robert Remini, *Andrew Jackson* (New York: HarperTrade, 1977).

Robert Remini, *The Battle of New Orleans: Andrew Jackson and America's First Military Victory* (New York: Viking Penguin, 1999).

Robert Remini, *The Course of American Democracy, 1833-1845, Vol 3* (Baltimore: Johns Hopkins University Press, 1998).

Robert Remini, *The Course of American Empire, 1767-1821, Vol. 1* (Baltimore: Johns Hopkins University Press, 1998).

Robert Remini, *The Course of American Freedom, 1822-1832, Vol 2* (Baltimore: Johns Hopkins University Press, 1998).

Robert Remini, *The Life of Andrew Jackson* (New York: Viking Penguin, 1990).

MARTIN VAN BUREN

Jim Hargrove, *Martin Van Buren: Eighth President of the United States* (Danbury, CT: Children's Press, 1988).

Robert Vincent Remini, *Martin Van Buren and the Making of the Democratic Party* (New York: Columbia University Press, 1959).

Martin Van Buren, *The Autobiography of Martin Van Buren* (New York: De Capo Press, 1973).

Major L. Wilson, *The Presidency of Martin Van Buren* (Lawrence: University Press of Kansas, 1984).

WILLIAM HENRY HARRISON AND JOHN TYLER

Paul Joseph, *William H. Harrison* (Edina, MN: ABDO Publishing Company, 2000).

Dee Lillegard, *John Tyler: Tenth President of the United States* (Danbury, CT: Children's Press, 1987).

Norma Lois Peterson, *Presidencies of William Henry Harrison and John Tyler* (Danbury, CT: Children's Press, 1987).

Anne Welsbacher, *John Tyler* (Edina, MN: ABDO Publishing Company, 2000).

JAMES K. POLK

Paul Bergeron, *The Presidency of James K. Polk* (Lawrence: University Press of Kansas, 1987).

Dee Lillegard, *James K. Polk: Eleventh President of the United States* (Danbury, CT: Children's Press, 1988).

Alison Tibbitts, *James K. Polk* (Springfield, NJ: Enslow Publishers, 1999).

ZACHARY TAYLOR AND MILLARD FILLMORE

K. Jack Bauer, *Zachary Taylor: Soldier, Planter, Statesman of the Old Southwest* (Baton Rouge: Louisiana State University Press, 1993).

Jane Clark Casey, *Millard Fillmore: Thirteenth President of the United States* (Danbury, CT: Children's Press, 1988).

Zachary Kent, *Zachary Taylor: Twelfth President of the United States* (Danbury, CT: Children's Press, 1988).

Elbert B. Smith, *The Presidencies of Zachary Taylor and Millard Fillmore* (Lawrence: University Press of Kansas, 1988).

FRANKLIN PIERCE

Larry Gara, *The Presidency of Franklin Pierce* (Lawrence: University Press of Kansas, 1991).

Charman Simon, *Franklin Pierce: Fourteenth President of the United States* (Danbury, CT: Children's Press, 1988).

Anne Welsbacher, *Franklin Pierce* (Edina, MN: ABDO Publishing Company, 2001).

JAMES BUCHANAN

David R. Collins, *James Buchanan: Fifteenth President of the United States.* (Ada, OK: Garrett Educational Corp., 1990).

Philip Shriver Klein, *President James Buchanan, A Biography* (University Park: Pennsylvania State University Press, 1962).

Elbert B. Smith, *The Presidency of James Buchanan* (Lawrence: University Press of Kansas, 1975).

ABRAHAM LINCOLN

David Herbert Donald, *Lincoln* (New York: Simon & Schuster Trade, 1996).

Russell Freedman, *Lincoln: A Photobiography* (New York: Clarion Books, 1987).

Mark E. Neely, *The Last Best Hope of Earth: Abraham Lincoln and the Promise of America* (Cambridge, Mass.: Harvard University Press, 1995).

Sterling North, *Abe Lincoln: Log Cabin to White House* (New York: Random House, Incorporated, 1987).

Stephen B. Oates, *Abraham Lincoln: The Man Behind the Myths* (New York: Harper Trade, 1993).

With Malice Toward None: The Life of Abraham Lincoln (New York: Harper Trade, 1993).

Carl Sandburg, *Abraham Lincoln: The Prairie Years and the War Years* (New York: Harcourt Brace & Company, 1974).

Augusta Stevenson, *Abraham Lincoln: Great Emancipator (Childhood of Famous Americans Series)* (New York: Simon & Schuster, 1988).

ANDREW JOHNSON

Albert E. Castel, *The Presidency of Andrew Johnson* (Lawrence: University Press of Kansas, 1993).

Martin Mantell, *Johnson, Grant, and the Politics of Reconstruction* (New York: Columbia University Press, 1973).

ULYSSES S. GRANT

Al Kaltman, *Cigars, Whiskey and Winning: Leadership Lessons from General Ulysses S. Grant* (New York: Prentice Hall Press, 2000).

Geoffrey Perret, *Ulysses S. Grant: Soldier and President (Modern Library Series)* (New York: Random House, Incorporated, 1998).

Brooks D. Simpson, *Ulysses S. Grant: Triumph Over Adversity* (New York: Houghton Mifflin Company, 2000).

RUTHERFORD B. HAYES

Art Hoogenboom, *The Presidency of Rutherford B. Hayes* (Lawrence: University Press of Kansas, 1988).

Zachary Kent, *Rutherford B. Hayes: Nineteenth President of the United States* (Danbury, CT: Children's Press, 1995).

Neal E. Robbins, *Rutherford B. Hayes: Nineteenth President of the United States* (Ada, OK: Garrett Educational Publishing, 1989).

JAMES GARFIELD AND CHESTER A. ARTHUR

Fern G. Brown, *James A. Garfield: 20th President of the United States* (Ada, OK: Garrett Educational Corp., 1990).

Justus D. Doenecke, *The Presidencies of James A. Garfield and Chester A. Arthur* (Lawrence: University Press of Kansas, 1981).

Paul Joseph, *Chester Arthur* (Edina, MN: ABDO Publishing Company, 2000).

Dee Lillegard, *James A. Garfield: Twentieth President of the United States* (Danbury, CT: Children's Press, 1987).

Charnan Simon, *Chester A. Arthur: Twenty-First President of the United States* (Danbury, CT: Children's Press, 1989).

GROVER CLEVELAND

Alan Brodsky, *Grover Cleveland: A Study in Character* (New York: St. Martin's Press, 2000).

David R. Collins, *Grover Cleveland: 22nd and 24th President of the United States* (Ada, OK: Garrett Educational Company, 1988).

H. Paul Jeffers, *An Honest President: The Life and Presidencies of Grover Cleveland* (New York: Morrow, William & Co., 2000).

Zachary Kent, *Grover Cleveland: Twenty-Second and Twenty-Fourth President of the United States* (Danbury, CT: Children's Press, 1988).

Richard E. Welch, *The Presidencies of Grover Cleveland* (Lawrence: University Press of Kansas, 1997).

BENJAMIN HARRISON

Susan Clinton, *Benjamin Harrison: Twenty-Third President of the United States* (Danbury, CT: Children's Press, 1989).

Paul Joseph. *Benjamin Harrison* (Edna, MN: ABDO Publishing Company, 1990).

Homer Edward Socolofsky, *The Presidency of Benjamin Harrison* (Lawrence: University Press of Kansas, 1987).

WILLIAM MCKINLEY

David R. Collins, *William McKinley: 25th President of the United States* (Ada, OK: Garrett Educational, 1990).

Lewis L. Gould, *The Presidency of William McKinley* (Lawrence: University Press of Kansas, 1981).

Paul Joseph, *William McKinley* (Edina, MN: ABDO Publishing Company, 2000).

THEODORE ROOSEVELT

George Grant, *Carry a Big Stick: The Uncommon Heroism of Theodore Roosevelt* (Nashville, TN: Cumberland House Publishing, 1996).

Nathan Miller, *Theodore Roosevelt: A Life* (New York: Morrow, William & Co., 1994).

Edmund Morris, *The Rise of Theodore Roosevelt* (New York: Random House, Incorporated, 1980).

Ed Winfield Parks, *Teddy Roosevelt: Young Rough Rider (The Childhood of Famous Americans Series)* (New York: Simon & Schuster Children's, 1989).

Henry Pringle, *Theodore Roosevelt: A Biography* (New York: Harcourt Brace & Company, 1972).

Dale L. Walker, *The Boys of '98: Theodore Roosevelt and the Rough Riders* (New York: St. Martinís Press, 1998).

WILLIAM HOWARD TAFT

Judith Icke Anderson, *William Howard Taft, An Intimate History* (New York: Norton, 1981).

Jane Clark Casey, *William Howard Taft: Twenty-Seventh President of the United States* (Danbury, CT: Children's Press, 1989).

Paolo Enrico Coletta, *The Presidency of William Howard Taft* (Lawrence: University Press of Kansas, 1973).

WOODROW WILSON

Louis Auchincloss, *Woodrow Wilson: A Penguin Lives Biography* (New York: Viking Penguin, 2000).

John Morton Blum, *Woodrow Wilson and the Politics of Morality* (Reading, MA.: Addison Wesley Longman, Inc., 1998).

Kendrick Clements, *The Presidency of Woodrow Wilson* (Lawrence: University of Kansas, 1992).

Alice Osinski, *Woodrow Wilson: Twenty-Eighth President of the United States* (Danbury, CT: Children's Press, 1989).

Arthur Walworth, *Woodrow Wilson* (New York: Norton, 1979).

WARREN G. HARDING

Anne Canadeo, *Warren G. Harding: 29th President of the United States* (Ada, OK: Garrett Educational, 1990).

Paul Joseph, *Warren G. Harding* (Edina, MN: ABDO Publishing Company, 2000).

Eugene P. Trani, *The Presidency of Warren G. Harding* (Lawrence: University Press of Kansas,???????).

Linda R. Wade, *Warren G. Harding: Twenty-Ninth President of the United States* (Danbury, CT: Children's Press, 1989).

CALVIN COOLIDGE

Calvin Coolidge, *The Autobiography of Calvin Coolidge* (Reprint Services Corporation, 1992).

Robert H. Ferrell, *The Presidency of Calvin Coolidge* (Lawrence: University Press of Kansas, 1998).

HERBERT HOOVER

Susan Clinton, *Herbert Hoover: Thirty-First President of the United States* (Danbury, CT: Children's Press, 1988).

Martin L. Fausold, *The Presidency of Herbert C. Hoover* (Lawrence: University Press of Kansas, 1994).

David M. Holford, *Herbert Hoover* (Springfield, NJ: Enslow Publishers, 1999).

FRANKLIN D. ROOSEVELT

Joseph Alsop, *FDR* (New York: Random House Value Publishing, Inc., 1998).

Russell Freedman, *Franklin Delano Roosevelt* (New York: Houghton Mifflin Company, 1992).

Frank Freidel, *Franklin D. Roosevelt: A Rendezvous With Destiny* (New York: Little, Brown & Company, 1991).

HARRY TRUMAN

Robert H. Ferrell, *Harry S. Truman: A Life* (Columbia: University of Missouri Press, 1996).

Alonzo L. Hamby, *Man of the People: A Life of Harry S. Truman* (New York: Oxford University Press, Incorporated, 1995).

Donald R. McCoy, *The Presidency of Harry S. Truman* (Lawrence: University Press of Kansas, 1990).

DWIGHT D. EISENHOWER

Stephen Ambrose, *Supreme Commander: The War Years of Dwight D. Eisenhower* (Garden City, NJ: Doubleday, 1970).

Robert F. Burlk, *Dwight D. Eisenhower, Hero and Politician* (Boston: Twayne Publishers, 1986).

Chester J. Pach, *The Presidency of Dwight D. Eisenhower* (Lawrence: University Press of Kansas, 1991).

JOHN F. KENNEDY

Anne Ayres, *The Wit and Wisdom of John F. Kennedy* (New York: Meridian Books, 1996).

Judy Donnelly, *Who Shot the President?: The Death of John F. Kennedy (Step into Reading Book)* (New York: Random House, Incorporated, 1988).

James Giglio, *The Presidency of John F. Kennedy* (Lawrence: University Press of Kansas, 1991).

Thomas C. Reeves, *A Question of Character: A Life of John F. Kennedy* (New York: Free Press, 1991).

LYNDON B. JOHNSON

Vaughn Davis Bornet, *The Presidency of Lyndon B. Johnson* (Lawrence: University Press of Kansas, 1984).

Robert Dallek, *Lone Star Rising: Lyndon Johnson and His Times, 1908-1960, Vol. 1* (New York: Oxford University Press, 1991).

Jim Hargrove, *Lyndon B. Johnson, Thirty-Sixth President of the United States* (Danbury, CT: Children's Press, 1987).

Anthony R. Kaye, *Lyndon B. Johnson* (Broomall, PA: Chelsea House Publishers, 1988).

Kurt Singer, *Lyndon Baines Johnson: A Man of Reason* (Minneapolis: T.S. Denison, 1964).

RICHARD NIXON

A&E Biography Video: *Richard Nixon: Man and President*.

Fred Emery, *Watergate: The Corruption of American Politics and the Fall of Richard Nixon* (New York: Simon & Schuster Trade Paperbacks, 1995).

Jeffrey P. Kimball, *Nixon's Vietnam War* (Lawrence: University Press of Kansas, 1998).

Melvin Small, *The Presidency of Richard Nixon* (Lawrence: University Press of Kansas, 1999).

GERALD FORD

James Cannon, *Time and Change: Gerald Ford's Appointment With History* (Ann Arbor, MI: University of Michigan Press, 1997).

David R. Collins, *Gerald R. Ford, 38th President of the United States* (Aa, OK: Garrett Educational, 1990).

John Robert Greene, *The Presidency of Gerald Ford* (Lawrence: University Press of Kansas, 1994).

Paul Joseph, *Gerald Ford* (Edina, MN: ABDO Publishing Company, 2000).

JIMMY CARTER

Jimmy Carter, *Keeping Faith: Memoirs of a President* (Little Rock: University of Arkansas Press, 1995).

Anne E. Schraff, *Jimmy Carter* (Springfield, NJ: Enslow Publishers, 1998).

Linda R. Wade, *James Carter: Thirty-Ninth President of the United States* (Danbury, CT: Children's Press, 1989).

RONALD REAGAN

A&E Biography Video: *Ronald Reagan: The Many Lives*.

Sarah Gallick, *Ronald Reagan: The Pictorial Biography* (Philadelphia, PA: Running Press Book Publishers, 1999).

Edmund Morris, *Dutch: A Memoir of Ronald Reagan* (New York: Random House, Incorporated, 1999).

GEORGE BUSH

Herbert S. Parmet, *George Bush: The Life of a Lone Star Yankee* (New York: Simon & Schuster Trade, 1997).

John Robert Greene, *The Presidency of George Bush* (University Press, 1999).

Jean Smith, *George Bush's War* (New York: Henry Holt, 1992).

BILL CLINTON

William Bennett, *The Death of Outrage: Bill Clinton and the Assault on American Ideals* (New York: Simon & Schuster, 1998).

David Maraniss, *First in His Class: A Biography of Bill Clinton* (New York: Simon & Schuster Trade Paperbacks, 1995).

Richard A. Posner, *An Affair of State: The Investigation, Impeachment, and Trial of President Clinton* (Cambridge, MA: Harvard University Press, 1999).

Susan Schmidt, *Truth at Any Cost: Ken Starr and the Unmaking of Bill Clinton* (New York: HarperCollins, 2000).

George Stephanopoulos, *All Too Human: A Political Education* (New York: Little, Brown & Company, 2000).